FOX TWO

The Story of America's First Ace in Vietnam

By
Randy Cunningham
with
Jeff Ethell

Champlin Fighter Museum

Library of Congress Catalog Number 83-27318
International Standard Book Number 0-912173-01-7
Printed and bound in the United States of America.

Library of Congress Cataloging in Publication Data

Cunningham, Randy, 1941 -
    Fox Two.

    Includes index.
    1. Vietnamese Conflict, 1961-1975 — Aerial operations,
American.   2. Cunningham, Randy, 1941-
3. Vietnamese Conflict, 1961-1975 — Personal narratives,
American.   4. Fighter pilots — United States — Biography.
5. United States. Navy — Officers — Biography.   I. Ethell,
Jeffrey L.   II. Title.   III. Title: Fox 2.
DS558.8.C86   1983   959.704'348   83-27318
ISBN 0-912173-01-7

Manuscript typed by Harriet Bowen

Dedicated to:

Randall Todd Cunningham
April Dianna Cunningham
Carrie Melissa Cunningham

CONTENTS

PREFACE

I am a fighter pilot by heart, and I love turning and twisting through the skies in search of a good fight. But this is more than a story of aerial combat. It is a story of a ship, USS *Constellation*, and the men who sailed her; their feelings, thoughts and actions during the Vietnam conflict.

Fox Two describes many of our air-to-air combats, recorded as they happened. We didn't win them all, but lessons learned and some of the restrictions that we had to live with — and in some cases die with — should be known by every American so that your sons will not pay the same price as did many of our men in a war we weren't allowed to win.

As our fighters twisted and turned in battle with the North Vietnamese MiGs over lush green jungle, the radio would be filled with cries of men locked in a life-and-death struggle for survival. Relative motion of fighter to fighter engaging head-on could reach speeds in excess of 2,000 miles per hour, or as little as zero. But little has changed since the time of Baron von Richthofen. Weapons systems have evolved, but air-to-air tactics and the dogfight still remain similar.

Our Navy and Air Force tactics utilize the concept of team fighting. The Navy used "loose deuce" tactics and the Air Force the "fluid four." The text will touch upon their significance, but for now the important factor is that many times the fighter pilot had to fire at an enemy aircraft in close proximity to a friendly. And your weapons system didn't know the good guy from the bad guy.

The radar-guided Sparrow missile (AIM-7E) was locked onto the target with pulse or pulse Doppler radar, selected either by the pilot or radar intercept officer in the F-4 Phantom. If my wingman was close to the enemy fighter, I had to be very careful not to lock up and select my wingman as the target. There was always a chance that the missile might guide to the wrong aircraft, so when firing the Sparrow the pilot called over the radio, "Fox One," to warn of an imminent Sparrow launch.

The Navy's most effective missile was the heat-seeking Sidewinder (AIM-9G). The Sidewinder, which could be fired inside 1,000 feet and over a mile, tracked the heat source of the enemy's tailpipe, but like the Sparrow was not selective of friendly or hostile. So when firing the Sidewinder the pilot called "Fox Two" to warn of the impending launch.

For example, if a MiG was chasing my wingman, both would most likely be using full afterburner. The F-4 had a hotter afterburner heat source than the MiGs, and with both MiG and wingman in my sight, it was difficult to fire, lest the missile kill my "wingie." When I called "Fox Two," it was a signal for him to deselect afterburner and make a break turn; if possible, in the direction to swing the MiG's tail toward the oncoming missile.

From 1965 through 1971 the US Navy scored 29 kills with Sidewinders. During the time period of this book, Navy pilots were credited with 23 Sidewinder kills and one Sparrow kill. All five of my victories were made with the Sidewinder, making Lieutenant (jg) Bill Driscoll and me the first US aces of the Vietnam War. Thus the title, *Fox Two*.

Randy Cunningham
Commander, US Navy

FOX TWO

Chapter 1

Connie —
USS *Constellation —*
through the
windscreen of an
approaching
helicopter in the
Tonkin Gulf during
1972.

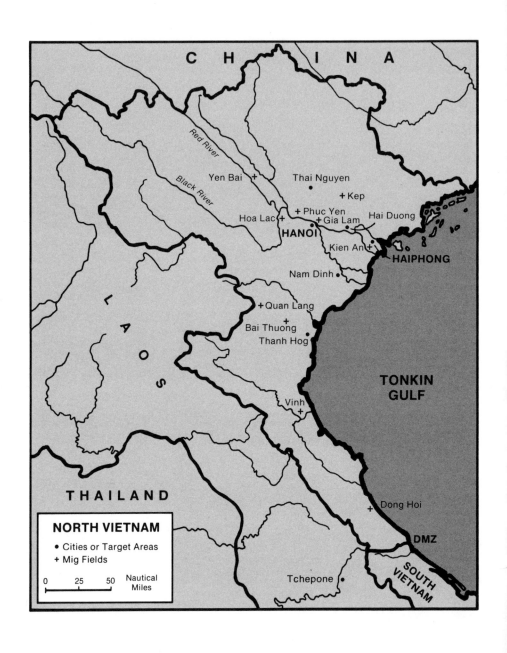

C H I N A

Red River

Black River

Yen Bai +

Thai Nguyen •

+ Kep

Hoa Lac +

+ Phuc Yen
+ Gia Lam   Hai Duong •

HANOI

Kien An +

HAIPHONG

Nam Dinh •

+ Quan Lang

+ Bai Thuong
Thanh Hog

L A O S

T O N K I N
G U L F

Vinh
+

T H A I L A N D

Dong Hoi
+

DMZ

Tchepone •

SOUTH
VIETNAM

NORTH VIETNAM

• Cities or Target Areas
+ Mig Fields

0   25   50   Nautical
Miles

CHAPTER 1
CONNIE UNDER PROTEST

The morning of October 1, 1971 was crystal clear as the men of USS *Constellation*, under the command of Captain J. D. Ward, prepared to get underway for the Western Pacific. The beginning of this second combat cruise would be a time of heartache for me. I honestly did not know if I would ever see my family again.

Amid public controversy and national news coverage, *Connie*, as we knew her, left San Diego harbor with an escort designed to protect the ship; protestors had set up picket lines around North Island, and public sentiment was mixed as several sailors refused to go to Vietnam and attempted to seek sanctuary in a nearby church. The protestors lauded their action but most of the men sailing had nothing but contempt for the confused young sailors.

After undergoing extensive training during our turnaround period, *Connie's* two fighter squadrons were sharp. The F-4 Phantom crews were combat-experienced and spoiling for a chance at the Russian-built MiGs.

During the first part of the air war over Vietnam in the 1960s, the pilots of the U.S. Navy and Air Force had been ill-trained and unprepared for close-in air-to-air fighting. Far too many pilots had been lost for the number of MiGs shot down.

I knew things would be different on this cruise. Navy fighter pilots had reached a level of proficiency perhaps equaled by no air force in the world, and each was confident he could top the enemy's fighters. Yet some would never return, while others would join their fellows in prison camps and prove to the Communists that a free mind cannot be controlled.

Halfway across the Pacific we dropped anchor among the shimmering beaches of Hawaii for a good four day's rest. We sailed from Pearl Harbor for the Philippine Islands and Subic Bay, our West Pacific home port. Despite the fun of liberty in the Philippines, much hard work was completed. Repairs were finished that couldn't be done at sea, supplies were taken on and *Connie* was made ready for our station in the Gulf of Tonkin.

Guss Eggert, Commander of Air Wing Nine aboard *Connie*, was confident of his squadrons as we joined *Enterprise* and *Coral Sea*, which already were conducting operations over Vietnam and Laos.

As the air wing prepared for combat in ever-increasing tempo, the enlisted men became personally involved. They knew that the pilots they helped into their planes would be facing tough resistance, but it was unusual for the crews to be so tense before our first mission. Reports of aircraft losses and heavy enemy anti-aircraft artillery continued to filter down the grapevine.

My first cruise, aboard *America*, had been relatively quiet since President Lyndon Johnson had restricted all bombing in North Vietnam. During that nine-month period in 1969-1970, the entire squadron had been fired upon only 12 times and very few of us had even seen a SAM. When I returned home to Shelbina, Missouri, where I had entered the world on December 8, 1941, the local newspaper printed, "Hero Returns." The only thing I had done was slow supplies through Laos and kill a few monkeys, certainly not enough to live up to my nickname, "Duke," which was patterned after one of my idols, John Wayne.

This time things were different. My roommate, Jim McKinney, and I were so restless that we spent most of the time fixing up our room. We had bought some green paint to cover our gray walls, only the color turned out to be a sickly pea-green.

Jim couldn't stand it. "Duke, we have to do something with this room. It's like living in a room full of spinach." Since Jim had purchased the paint, assuring me it would dry darker, I told him to see what he could do to fix it up. We couldn't mess it up any more.

A few hours later Jim came up all excited and said, "Duke, just wait till you see what I've done for our room." Walking down the passageway I found a bunch of guys inside our room laughing their heads off. Jim had painted the trim around everything ... orange. At least it wasn't the dullest room on the ship.

Entering Strike Operations just before our first mission gave me a joltingly unpleasant surprise. The chart marking the known AAA and SAM locations with color-coded pins looked like a Christmas tree. A year before the chart had been virtually absent of pins.

The Gomers, as someone had nicknamed the North Vietnamese early in the war, meant business. They had moved SAM sites south of the DMZ and into Laos. Many of the guns that had once fortified North Vietnam were moved south with the apparent notion that the United States would never resume bombing the North.

The supply route that had once consisted of Gomers walking and carrying equipment piece by piece had changed into a highly complex logistical network. Trucks had taken the place of bicycles; bulldozers etched out hundreds of roads beneath jungle covering. Tanks and troops readily moved southward and their gunners had more shells than they needed.

I had prepared myself to meet the threat of MiGs but I wasn't counting on being shot at by more than small arms fire. Now we would face 23mm, 37mm, 57mm, 85mm, 100mm, 120mm and SAMs on every mission. I had no idea that we were to drop more bombs during the first two weeks of combat than we had on the previous nine-month cruise.

Our first mission was near the valley of Tchepone in Laos, the subject of a song written by Air Force fighter pilot Toby Hughes. On the way across the pond all of us had joked about the lyrical horrors of this song since it was posted in our readyroom. When the strike leader marked an X over our assigned target of Tchepone, the laughing stopped.

The Gomers were infiltrating heavily through the Tchepone Valley. Supply trucks lined the roads and enemy defenses had been increased to protect supplies streaming in from Russia and China by way of transport ships in the gulf ports.

The room grew quiet as plans for the strike were laid out. Four F-4 Phantoms, four A-6 Intruders and four A-7 Corsairs would rendezvous with an OV-10 forward air controller, call sign Covey 632. Each flight of four aircraft — the small formations to afford us better maneuverability when fired upon — would proceed through a corridor just north of Da Nang Air Base. We could not overfly North Vietnam, and the corridor afforded us safe passage into Laos, most of which was under enemy control and crammed with air defense systems. The enemy had moved most of his guns out of the north to protect supply routes such as the Ho Chi Minh Trail.

Lieutenant Brian Grant, my assigned wingman, looked at me and asked, "Is this guy kidding or is he just trying to scare us? Everyone told us how easy the last cruise turned out to be." I leaned over and told Brian to plan for the worst — it's always better to be prepared than surprised. His RIO, Lieutenant Jerry "Sea Cow" Sullivan, and I had seen combat, and we knew what lay ahead. But this would be the first time in combat for Brian and my RIO, Lieutenant (jg) Bill "Irish" Driscoll. The Navy normally placed an experienced pilot with a "nugget" backseater or vice-versa to reduce the possibility of error and to prevent aircraft losses. Regardless, we all felt uneasy.

The weather briefer was next: "It will be clear, but expect a dense haze created from the farmers' burning their rice stalks after harvest." The haze decreased visibility, making it difficult at times to find our targets. The intelligence briefer, whom we had nicknamed "Spook" due to all his spooky facts culled from previous missions, pinpointed the best route in and out, marking friendly-held areas if we had to bail out. The only trouble with friendly areas was their lack of reliability.

MiG attack was unlikely, but possible threat areas were always planned for just in case the Gomers got frisky. Our major concern was AAA and SAMs. The Vietnamese were masters of camouflage and they constantly moved their defenses; no telling where the guns and missiles would be this day. Spook marked known AAA positions and recommended run-in headings taking into account sun and terrain.

We figured each mission like a trip to Las Vegas. To beat the odds required planning. The better the planning, the better the chance of a successful mission and safe return. Each mission demanded hours of planning and briefing, the problems demanding separate attention in turn. There was room for nothing but a professional attitude among the aircrews.

Lieutenant "Quack" Reinheld, M.D., looked after our physical and mental problems, and I'm sure he prevented many accidents by his watchful eye. To each of us who were to fly he passed morphine packets, which we fervently hoped wouldn't be needed, and salt tablets to combat the heat.

There were no pep talks, no propaganda lectures. Each man in his own heart had to rationalize his reasons for being there. As for me, the issue was not complicated. I had been ordered by my commander-

An F-4J prepares to launch from *Constellation* as the catapult crewmen adjust the cables.

in-chief to defend the rights of the Vietnamese people, whom I believe deserved those rights just as the South Koreans, Israelis, Cubans and Chinese deserve theirs. We were fighting a totalitarian ideology fueled by the Soviet Union. The Soviets had been slowly removing freedom from the world for a long time, causing much of the turmoil on our planet. Russia was against us then and Russia will be against us in the future.

We co-ordinated our strike plans and prepared ourselves for the mission. The chaplain had a last shot at us, preparing us in another much-needed way.

As we put the final touches on our plans, the plane captains were feverishly preparing our aircraft. Often I got so busy I forgot that other people besides pilots have feelings. These young men, many just out of high school, were loading bombs, fueling planes, preparing catapults and themselves for the ordeal ahead.

As I walked through the hangar deck, smiling faces greeted me. The troops hadn't asked to be there anymore than we had, and before year's end a few of them would be dead. They were just kids, but they never complained, never slacked in their work. Often these enlisted guys lifted my spirits by their dedication and relentless effort. I was proud to be part of such a team, as were all the men aboard *Constellation*.

Irish called my room. "Time to get ready, Duke." A quick check of our flight gear and survival equipment, a last-minute joke with the other crews to break the silence as we made our way topside, a tender pat of my rabbit's foot. Brian jumped as the deck crew fired a practice catapult; no load, but steam hissed through the slots of the deck as in a live shot.

As we stepped into the sunlight I squinted at the piercing brightness. Thankfully the Tonkin Gulf's hot, moist air had been turned into a cool breeze by the ship's movement into the wind. Lieutenant George Gorianick, leader of the A-7s, shouted "Hey, Duke," and gave me the finger as a broad smile crossed his face. George was as big as a rhino with a temperament to match when it came to the opposition. He could lay a 1,000-pound bomb into a tea cup, though he would have preferred a beer mug. George's biggest dream was to get a MiG with his A-7 and put the fighters to shame. And he almost did it on May 10, 1972.

Our plane captain was taking pictures of Irish and me as we

Simultaneous launch of a VF-96 Phantom and an A-7E off *Connie's* bow as other A-7s and A-6s await their turn.

preflighted our Phantom. I hammed it up and struck a pose walking to the front of the aircraft. Next thing I knew, Irish was standing over me: I had tripped over a tie-down chain and fallen flat on my rear. With bruised dignity I picked myself up and tried not to look at the rest of the flight-deck crew shaking their heads.

Our F-4 was ready. The ground crews had done a good job — now it was our turn. I remember the look on Irish's face as he climbed up the ladder and said, "Go get 'em Duke, I'll be right behind you." Like the Indy 500 a voice blared out over the loudspeaker, "Start your engines." *Connie* turned her skirts into the wind, giving us about 30 knots across the deck to help us get airborne during the cat shot.

Canopies closed as the furnace-like heat burst from the jet engines. Sweat poured down my face. The deck crews launched the A-6 tanker and motioned us onto the catapult. I looked down the cat toward the pointy end of the ship and saw the ocean 60 feet below. Irish set the ejection sequence handle. The catapult officer lifted his right hand in the air, pointed his index finger and motioned for 100% power. The F-4 strained forward on the hold-back bridle. Then the signal was given to select full afterburner. The air conditioning system blasted into our sweaty faces. A quick final check by the cat officer . . . he saluted and we returned the traditional affectionate finger. Leaning down to touch the deck with two fingers, the signal was given by the cat officer for the catapult operator to fire us off. The G force was so great my vision blurred, but it was a good shot and we were free to hunt like an eagle.

"Go ahead, Duke, I'm right behind you!" Lieutenant (jg) William "Willie" Driscoll was my radar intercept officer, and sure enough, he always was right behind me in our Phantom.

Chapter 2

Connie's flight deck crewmen direct an E-2B of VAW-116 into position for launch. The Hawkeye was aptly named, serving as "eyes of the fleet" with long-range radar and early warning gear.

CHAPTER 2
DEATH RUNS DEEP

Gear and flaps up . . . the F-4 was accelerating smoothly as I turned back for rendezvous. I never ceased to wonder at the catapult's ability to get my 56,000-pound fighter airborne in a matter of seconds, particularly on a hot, sticky November day like this one.

Looking back over my shoulder I saw Brian and Sea Cow joining to get on my wing as we flew back over the ship. After Brian gave the signal that everything checked out, we pushed throttles forward and accelerated to our 400-knot climb speed, leveling off at 20,000 feet.

Having Brian on my wing gave me a sense of comfort and excitement all mixed into one. He was a good tactition and a super "stick" (pilot; RIOs were "scopes"). I didn't want some lieutenant commander or commander as a wingman. Many of the senior officers just wanted to be sure to make it back . . . I wanted someone nearby who was as excited as I was about downing MiGs. Not that I didn't want to get back too, but "why let rank lead, when ability can do it better?"

All the junior officers gaining altitude over the gulf that day reflected the finest in the fleet. Our squadron, VF-96, would go on to win the Adm. Joseph Clifton Award for the best fighter squadron in the Navy twice in a row, earning the right to paint the coveted "E" for excellence on our aircraft. I felt proud to be flying with the Fighting Falcons.

As we neared the corridor just north of Da Nang, each flight had to check in with a shore controlling agency, coded Hillsborough. The UHF radios popped into life: "Hillsborough, this is Showtime; two Fox Fours, level 20K, six Mark 82s (500 pound bombs) per aircraft; our mission number 631."

Hillsborough then looked at his tactical board updated by the forward air controllers assigned to various sections south of the DMZ.

"Showtime," Hillsborough responded, "rendezvous the 280° radial for 100 nautical miles Hue Tacan radio. Fix and contact Covey 632 on 303.0" The FAC, Covey 632, had spotted three trucks passing throught the Chapone Valley, camouflaged alongside the road.

We hit our coast-in point and headed 270° for approximately 70 miles to avoid the restricted areas, then turned north toward Tchepone. With Brian on my left wing we paralleled the North Vietnamese border. He said he felt a bit more comfortable on that side since the threat area was to our right.

Approaching the assigned rendezvous point, all of us scanned the jungle floor. FACs normally flew above 3,000 feet to keep themselves out of small-arms fire range. Their OV-10 Broncos plodded along at just over 100 knots and, even though enemy gunners held their fire for the jets most of the time, if a FAC ventured too close he was in for a barrage. Those FAC crews really had our admiration.

With his upper wing painted white, Covey was easy to spot . . . right where he was scheduled to be and ready for action. "Showtime, I've got three trucks for you parked alongside the road."

It sounded simple, but the VC were not stupid. They had truck stops surrounded by AAA sites just waiting for us to roll in.

"Showtime," Covey came back, "give me two runs north to south with instantaneous fusing, then make your pull up to the south." Instantaneous fusing threw 90% of the bomb blast above the ground, destroying anything around for a healthy radius. We also used delayed fuses, allowing the bombs to penetrate deep into the surface before exploding, creating large craters or landslides.

The south pull-up would bring us over the high karst mountains, our best santuary from the VC if we were hit by ground fire and forced to eject. If I were going to punch out, I wanted all the help I could get until the rescue choppers arrived. Yet I recall countering those thoughts by remembering we had always been warned of AAA on the previous cruise, but had only milk runs. I don't think any of us let ourselves think that we would be the ones to get it . . . it was always someone else.

Circling at 15,000 feet, we watched Covey go into action. The light propeller-driven aircraft nosed over into a steep dive, heading for trucks we couldn't ever hope to spot from this altitude. He fired a smoke rocket that hit 10 meters south of the trucks, but by the time Brian and I flew around a large cloud the smoke had dissipated due to high surface winds.

We asked for a second rocket and a sharp, crackling Air Force voice burst from the UHF, "Come on, you Navy pukes, I don't have all day!" and once again he arced over toward the target.

This time little white puffs of 37mm AAA appeared all around the OV-10. I called out, "Covey, they are shooting all around you . . . look out!" He kept pressing into the target, placing a rocket smack in the middle of trucks.

With relief I watched his nose start pulling skyward. "Okay, Navy," Covey radioed, "the score is six to nothing; Air Force six, Navy. . ."

The Bronco erupted into flame as a 37mm made a direct hit! I sat there in utter horror . . . I had never watched an airplane shot down. Helplessness washed over me in sickening waves. As he hit the jungle floor, rage poured into me. . ."That damn gun is opening up on us!"

Two A-7s had joined our orbiting flight and the lead Corsair called out, "I see the gun flashes." In seconds he was down and in the slot for a run. The bombs pickled off with uncanny accuracy. They must have hit the gun and its ammunition dump. Secondary explosions rocked the jungle floor.

For the first time in my life I really wanted to kill someone. Brian and I rolled in, putting our bombs square on the trucks, but nothing could be done for the Air Force FAC. My guts ached as I flew over the burning aircraft looking for signs of life.

Our fuel was low and Air Force F-4s were now overhead directing search and rescue efforts, so we headed back toward *Connie*. We never found out if the FAC made it or not.

As we cruised back to the ship I was alone in my thoughts. Our first day and all hell had let loose. What were we in for? How many more aircraft would I see go down? Would I get used to it?

Coming back aboard *Connie* there was no relief at returning safely. I was sickened knowing someone back home would soon receive a letter from the Defense Department.

Drenched in sweat, I crawled out of the airplane and walked in a daze to the ready room. As I entered there was silence. We all felt the same. Our section was scheduled for another strike later in the day...

Armed for both strike and air-to-air missions, a "Fighting Falcon" F-4J of VF-96 carries six bombs and four Sidewinder missiles.

we could hardly wait to give the enemy a taste of our revenge. It may sound bad, but that's what we felt at the time.

The first days of combat rolled by as the air wing settled into a routine. The two F-4 squadrons, my own VF-96 and VF-92, were assigned four basic missions: bombing, photo escort, BARCAP or fleet combat air patrol, and flak supression. The majority of the Phantom sorties fell into the latter two.

Normally the air superiority mission of escorting RA-5 Vigilantes on photo reconnaissance runs over the north was uneventful, but there were certainly exceptions.

My first photo run was for a Vigilante driven over Vinh airfield by Commander Murph Wright. He never got slower than 500 knots. I fully expected to be fired upon but it was quiet and almost peaceful below.

With a false sense of security, I was assigned to make the same run the next day. No sooner had we hit the coast then the sky filled with black puffs from the tracking AAA sites. Nearing Vinh the electronic countermeasures (ECM) gear lit up the cockpit — the enemy was busy getting ready for something.

"SAMs!"

My stomach contracted in honest-to-goodness fear, a reaction I would never lose at a SAM call. Sweat came pouring out of both Willie (a nickname I often traded with Irish) and me.

The Vigie driver broke toward one SAM and defeated it with a high-G maneuver. The second one was after us.

"Duke, SAM at three o'clock!" Willie called out.

I could see the RA-5 heading on its way — I'd have to leave him and deal with the missile. I turned to starboard and the approaching white pencil corrected toward us. I broke port . . . so did the missile. It was locked onto us and tracking.

I was in full afterburner — 36,000 pounds of thrust was accelerating the F-4 to 600 knots. I was tense, too tense. My hand was almost numb from gripping the control stick. Willie and I both kept our eyes on the SAM as it came closer and closer — my mouth was drying up. Holding the fighter at zero G, or unloaded, as we called it, I was counting on breaking at the last moment. We broke hard into the SAM and it couldn't turn the corner. We could see the fins moving as it passed by like a snake strike. The Gomers had failed to get us today, but there was always tomorrow. Our Phantom made it to the Gulf without further incident.

No matter how many SAMs a pilot might defeat, he respected them. Each SAM call brought doubts of survival and numbing fear. They were never faced complacently.

The enemy's airfields were always to the north, beyond the reach of *Connie*'s radar. ECM aircraft were placed on the outer limits of the ship's radar capability, giving greater coverage for our missions. Loaded with four heat-seeking Sidewinders and four radar-guided Sparrows, our F-4s would patrol outside the 12-mile coastal limit between the MiG fields and the carrier. These BARCAP, or fleet protection flights against outbound MiGs or patrol boats, were long and often boring. Even though the MiGs might be flying over the coast only a few miles away, we were restricted from intercepting them unless they posed a threat to the fleet.

Brian and I preferred to fly 100 feet above the water to hide from the coastal radars. There was never a time when North Vietnamese fishing fleets would not blanket the Gulf. Keeping our speed high, we would often pass directly between these ships — the people on board would wave, but we varied our flight path since some of the junks were armed with light machine guns. To my knowledge, however, the fishermen never shot at us. It was not unusual to see 15 to 20 people crowded onto one small boat miles from shore, all wearing the traditional black pajamas. I sometimes wondered what they thought of enemy aircraft flying so close to them. What were the people really like? I would welcome the opportunity to go back and talk to some of them, though I'm glad I never personally found out if they were just hard-working fishermen or hard-core VC.

Other ships pulled into the North's many harbors daily... French, Chinese, Russian. SAMs, fuel, trucks, amunition, MiG crates and other supplies were easy to spot on their decks. Because of political strings we were forbidden to touch these obvious war supplies. I wish some of the people who controlled those strings would fly just once on the receiving end over a heavily defended target.

Christmas Day 1971 was only a few weeks away, but no one felt much like celebrating. In just a short span of time we had seen too much ...

One of VF-92's pilots had returned from a mission with one engine out and a hydraulic failure. It would have been no sweat for him to fly to Da Nang and rest until the aircraft was repaired, but the fighter pilot's "can do" attitude prevailed.

He made one pass at the deck in an attempt to land, but with his hydraulic malfunction and the configuration of his aircraft, he came in with too much speed, landing half way down the deck and missing all four arresting wires. As he boltered, he added full power and went around.

His second try was much like the first, forcing another go-around. He was determined to try again. As he made the turn into the ship he called, "I don't think I can make it." Those were his last words. The F-4 stalled as he tried to pull the already slow Phantom around the corner. The wing dropped right as the RIO ejected, but the pilot didn't make it.

The tension aboard ship was mounting. Each mission was more dangerous than the last as the enemy brought in larger AAA and moved SAM sites into Laos and South Vietnam.

I remember finding the passageways alive with activity one night when everyone should have been trying to relax. The attack pilots were cutting up maps of North Vietnam. Making my way to the readyroom I got in on the announcement: for the first time in three years we were going to strike North Vietnam.

There were mixed emotions on the faces of my buddies. . . and within myself. Most of us felt it was about time we stopped pussyfooting around and stopped the enemy cold, as we should have done some seven years earlier. On the other hand, this meant higher risks — many of us would not come back. No one balked at going. We were ready to do our best.

Among the F-4 crews there was a high-strung undertone that transcended fear. . . we would be in range of the MiG bases. Air-to-air combat was a trained fighter pilot's ultimate goal, and VF-96 pilots were good.

By December the war had taken on an even grimmer outlook. More and more supplies were making it down the trail. We were hurting the VC with our strikes, but they were still getting enough men, weapons and supplies to give our ground forces a very rough time.

First the Air Force B-52s began to bring their awesome weight against the flow of traffic. The destruction wrought by a section of Stratofortresses was the most feared weapon we had, according to captured VC. Ultimately the '52s earned the lion's share in bringing North Vietnam to the negotiating tables.

As we prepared for our first mission over the North, the mission

Air Wing Nine was composed of squadrons which didn't always get the attention they deserved. Here a Phantom of VF-92 is catapulted off the angled deck while A-7s of VA-146 and 147 turn up prior to locking wings and taxiing into position.

briefings made it clear that we would be flying under strict control. Strike areas had to be memorized in order to avoid bombing the wrong target or civilian settlements. Any deviation from assigned targets would be dealt with severely. Fighter Squadron 96 was to go to Vinh airfield and the supply routes leading south.

We studied inbound and outbound routes and known threat areas. Survival gear must have been checked by everyone a dozen times, particularly the small emergency radios and signaling devices in case of a shoot-down.

Evening Mass was overcrowded. There wasn't much said among the men as we thought of the eternal things of God. The enlisted men worked on through the night loading bombs and air-to-air missles. Some of the ordnance guys chalked their names and suitable greetings on some of the bombs.

I didn't get much sleep. When first light appeared the sky was filled with rain and heavy seas. It would have been next to impossible to launch a strike in that stuff.

Sure enough, upon entering the ready room we found the strike had been cancelled, but not due to weather. Washington's approval to hit the North had not been finalized. Morale took a plunge. It almost would have been better if we had gone since everyone was hacked off at having been put through the tension of a false alarm. Regardless, we all knew we were going to go shortly, along with the rest of the Navy and Air Force in the area. It couldn't have been soon enough as far as we were concerned.

One of the most sophisticated aircraft in Naval Aviation during the Vietnam War was the RA-5C Vigilante. This "Vigie" belonged to another Air Wing Nine squadron, RVAH-11, beginning a photo-recon mission in April 1972.

Chapter 3

The natives were restless Up North. After flying over Laos and South Vietnam early in our 1972 tour, where flak and ground fire constituted the main threats, we had to cope with surface-to-air missiles. Here a SAM has exploded over the Red River Valley.

CHAPTER 3
OPERATION PROUD DEEP

As the orders came through for resumed bombing of North Vietnam in late 1971, it was obvious that the United States was intending to make use of its airpower. The Navy was slated to strike coastal interdiction points, MiG fields and supply storage areas. The Air Force was to concentrate on inland targets while the South Vietnamese Air Force would provide close air support to their troops. The recce photos uncovered large supply stockpiles in each target area — millions of gallons of fuel oil, tanks, SAMs, launchers and military equipment lay out in the open awaiting shipment south. It seemed the enemy was confident the U.S. would never re-enter the North.

Again preparations were made for a major strike from *Connie*. All 40 aircraft from the strike group rendezvoused over the ship — A-7 and A-6 bombers, KA-3 and KA-6 tankers, missile suppression aircraft, flak suppressors and fighters, all in formation waiting for the code word to execute. The Gulf's weather was bad as we went up above the cloud layers.

Two A-7 Corsairs were sent to check weather conditions over Vinh airfield as we waited. The sight was fascinating... the sky a brilliant blue with 40 Navy jets in formation silhouetted against white clouds. And I was getting a breathtaking view from my perch above the force as fighter cover. Previously our strike forces consisted of four Phantoms going into Laos... there was no comparison to what I was seeing now.

I wasn't lost in the silent serenity of formated airplanes for long. As the A-7s went feet dry over the beach the radio came to life: "Busy Bee, SAM, SAM, three o'clock; Busy Bee, two more at 12 o'clock, break port; one at nine and tracking."

Our eyes were fixed toward the scene of action. Smoke trails from the SAMs broke through into the sunlit sky! My heart was beating so fast I was sure it was going to pop into my lap. A glance at Willie in the rearview mirror — he didn't look too happy either; then over at Brian hugging my wing — he just shook his head.

The Corsairs made it out without a scratch, reporting the weather was too poor for effective completion of the mission. We were ordered to RTB (return to base). Once again we had prepared ourselves for the worst, only to go through the letdown of cancellation.

After coming back aboard, the crews gathered in strike operations to get word on what was going to happen if the poor weather continued. No one wanted to believe what they heard. We were going to fly using the A-6 computer and radar systems to locate the targets above the 12,000-foot overcast. The strike aircraft would fly wing on the A-6 — when his bombs were dropped we would drop simultaneously from straght and level a few thousand feet above the clouds.

From 1965 to '67 the planners had learned the lesson of never attacking above an overcast, let alone of flying a predictable path at subsonic speeds and allowing the AAA and SAM radars to pinpoint the formations for a firing solution. Instrument weather tactics were unthinkable in a low-threat area and a double hazard over the North.

All this didn't seem to make much difference. Either the Navy and Air Force would complete Operation Proud Deep in the allotted time or cancel. A tactical risk was chosen with an increased loss rate to divert a possible Viet Cong offensive. We went on to take our licks, losing 26 aircraft in five days.*

Our first instrument bombing mission consisted of the A-6s with a small group of A-7s and F-4s flying wing on each one. My VF-96 had assigned two Phantoms to each strike group.

Lieutenant Steve Shoemaker and his wingman were assigned to the first Intruder while Brian and I attached ourselves to the second. Steve's RIO, Keith Crenshaw, was one of the funniest guys I have had the pleasure of meeting. We nicknamed him "Cannonball" for his short, round body and comical, direct sense of humor. What a pair they made — "Shoe" was a tall, gangly six feet, "Cannonball"

*Tactical analysis of post-strike information revealed that damage to enemy logistics was minimal. Bad weather plus newly-tried systems failed to bring about acceptable results.

short and squatty. They looked like Abbot and Costello. Cannonball made it clear he wouldn't feel too bad if the A-6 "broke" (was found unserviceable) on the deck.

We flew to a preassigned spot in the Gulf, north of the target. My SAM warning gear indicated we were being scanned by enemy radar; no doubt we were pinpointed.

The first strike element with Shoemaker detached from the main body and headed in toward the target. Our position was charted as safe, since no known SAM sites had been observed, yet after 60° of turn my warning system indicated a SAM launch!

"No joy" on the missile . . . it was somewhere in the clouds. I remember thinking, "I told you so, damn it!"

Ten miles away F-4s from another carrier were over Vinh. Suddenly the air was full of missiles! One Phantom was hit, transforming itself into a flaming torch. Two parachutes blossomed... the two crewmen, Dave Hoffman and Norris Charles, were taken prisoners.

Fixation on the other strike group didn't last long. Our hidden SAM came winging by the lead strike formation. Then the A-6 pilot called for the A-7 to take the lead; a radar system had malfunctioned.

The Corsair accelerated and took the element lead as a second missile emerged from the overcast, heading for Shoe! I felt like I had marbles in my mouth as I croaked out, "Steve, SAM, one o'clock low!"

"Tally Ho, I've got it, Duke."

He immediately commenced his SAM evasion maneuvering. I heard Cannonball call out, "Pull this damn thing, Shoe; it's getting close!"

The missile went over the top of his F-4 and headed for the A-6.

Shoe reversed and gave a warning call to the A-6 pilot. No reaction. Another frantic call to the A-6 driver, but he still had only 20° angle of bank and two Gs on his aircraft.

Again that utterly helpless feeling washed over me as I watched a friend in trouble. I held my breath, watching the missile close in. It was like watching a car about to hit a child and not being able to help.

A tremendous fireball... my mind exploded, "Oh my God, he's dead!"

Another SAM was on the way up. Things were happening too fast. I broke away from our A-6 and accelerated to 550 knots. With the coolness of a professional, Steve called for me to join him. The confusion in my mind began to settle. Steve was giving orders to the other strike birds to set up a search and rescue force for the downed

Attack Squadron 165 flew the A-6 Intruder from *Constellation*, providing all-weather, day or night strike capability.

A-6 crew. Downed A-6 crew? I couldn't believe they had made it out of that flaming mess.

We punched our F-4s down through the overcast, breaking out underneath. North Vietnamese boats were all over the place.

An A-7 pilot found one of the survivors, the navigator, between the mainland and a cluster of islands. VC boats were wasting no time in trying to reach him. Moving in to get close, our formation was fired upon by gunners on the islands. It must have been quite a sight under that low scud — the entire strike group had diverted to commence an all-out effort to rescue both crewmen. When one of us was downed, the entire war stopped as everything was done to effect a rescue. Knowing this was a tremendous morale booster, especially sitting in enemy waters surrounded by hostile vessels.

The A-7 strafed the gun positions, forcing the gunners to divert their fire toward him. Aerial tankers were already overhead to supply extra fuel for the effort as more F-4s patrolled for MiGs.

When the rescue helos started to press in for their initial try at picking up our guy, intense AAA fire forced them back. Two A-7 pilots deliberately flew right on top of the enemy guns, drawing enough fire to enable a helo to reach the downed navigator and get out. By any standard it was a heroic effort though there was remorse over loss of the pilot — he was never found.

Shoe and I still had our 500-pound bombs. As the rescue was in progress we spotted three large boats heading for the navigator. We made one warning pass in an attempt to turn them back. That was a mistake — they opened fire on us as we flew by. The next run would be no warning.

Our bombs hit in the middle of one boat, leaving pieces no bigger than toothpicks. We pulled up and circled. The remaining boats turned back toward sanctuary. We headed for *Connie*.

That evening we visited the rescued navigator in the hospital ward and asked why the A-6 didn't break to avoid the SAM. As it turned out, the pilot never saw it. The force of the explosion ejected the navigator and the only thing he remembered was floating through the clouds in his chute. He had suffered some internal injuries, a broken arm plus first-, second- and third-degree burns, but he was mighty happy to be back with us.

MiGs were never much of a problem during Proud Deep even though they were flying out of Kep, Phuc Yen, Yen Bai and Bai

Every bombing mission has to start with ordnance and handlers. Young men such as these were instrumental in Air Wing Nine's outstanding record compiled over Laos, South and North Vietnam.

Thuong and occasionally out of Vinh and Quan Lang. They had an aversion to jumping any strike force where the odds did not favor them.

It's very difficult to look back on the whole thing and not give vent to feelings of frustration. Proud Deep was very costly to both the Air Force and the Navy. We flew under the most hazardous of situations, garnering poor bombing results with loss of aircrew killed or taken prisoner.

Since the commencement of the air war in 1964, the effort was one characterized by restriction on all quarters. Weather conditions favored the enemy, and Washington's control of the war from afar severely limited our ability to react flexibly. Enemy sancturaries in Cambodia were off-limits, even though we knew the enemy was operating from these base camps.

Haiphong, the key port through which 85% of North Vietnam's imports flowed, was not mined until May of 1972. Then when we *were* allowed to bomb some of the ports, it was at night under overcast skies, illuminated by flares which proved ideal for the enemy gunners!

President Johnson's speech of April 7, 1965 seemed hollow: "Our objective is the independence of South Vietnam and its freedom from attack. . . We will do everything necessary to reach that objective, and we will do only what is absolutely necessary. . .

"We will not be defeated. . .

"We will not grow tired. . .

"We will not withdraw, either openly or under the cloak of a meaningless agreement. . . and we will remain ready. . . for unconditional discussion."

Operation Proud Deep and Operation Linebacker (the B-52 strikes in December 1972), like Operation Rolling Thunder early in the war, were designed to strangle the enemy's logistical supply system until Hanoi capitulated. But our own politicians saw to it that the war waned by allowing only spasmodic attacks against the North. Each time we started hurting North Vietnam, Hanoi would cry out to the world. Sanctuary zones were placed around Haiphong and Hanoi. Only the stand by President Nixon in 1972 drew Hanoi to the negotiating table after our B-52s pounded these two key targets.

In December 1971 and throughout the war, operations were conducted with specific guidance from the highest levels of government. Squadron commanders were told which day and hour to

Other unheralded but essential members of *Connie's* winning team were the plane captains and mechanics who kept our birds in the air. Here one of our A-7 pilots discussed the status of his Corsair II with some of the maintenance folks.

strike, regardless of weather conditions and the safety of our pilots. We were told the number of sorties we could perform on the assigned target, what type of ordnance to use and, at times, the direction of attack.

Only military trucks moving on the roads could be bombed from 20,000 feet. I still haven't figured out how to tell a military truck from a so-called commercial truck while being fired at by AAA and SAMs. If the trucks contained SAM launchers or other war materials and were parked in a village, they could not be bombed.

After President Johnson's announcement to cease the bombing of the North, Hanoi grabbed the opportunity to spend those few years until late 1971 building up its defense system in the North, South and in Laos. Radar networks were moved as far south as the DMZ; AAA and SAMs were set up on a wide scale. Russia increased North Vietnam's supply of MiG fighters and accelerated pilot training in Communist-bloc countries.

Then we received orders not to shoot at a MiG unless fired upon first! Hell, whoever wrote that one never flew air-to-air combat!

That rule extended to all targets in North Vietnam. If a missile site, AAA emplacement or military installation fired upon our forces engaged in a strike near the border in Laos, or fired upon an unarmed reconnaissance aircraft, it was okay to shoot back. Otherwise, leave them alone. More political rules that tied our hands and got many of our pilots killed. Out of this came the term "protective reaction strike."

To counter this revolting set of circumstances, each recce mission was escorted by a large strike group. When the photo bird was fired upon, the enemy position was destroyed.

The press back home claimed that Air Force and Navy pilots were bombing the North indiscriminately and without authorization. To my knowledge, we never struck anything in the North unless we were fired upon first.

The enemy's logistical supply route was directed through the mountain passes leading into Laos. We would bomb trucks coming out of these passes as they crossed into Laos, hopefully before they reached the Laotian jungle. Guns and SAM sites were located along mountain ridges and each time our planes attacked truck convoys, missiles would pop up out of nowhere. It was militarily to their advantage and they capitalized on it until we were allowed to do something about it.

During my two years in Southeast Asia we never crossed the Laotian border into the North without first being fired upon... and always from the Laotian side.

Chapter 4

This is a fortuitous
photograph, as it shows the
two F-4Js in which Willie
and I scored our five MiG
kills. In number 112 we
bagged a MiG-21 on
19 January 1972 and a 17
on 8 May. We flew number
100 on 10 May when we
shot down three 17s.

CHAPTER 4
MY FIRST KILL

During the first months of 1972 North Vietnamese MiG activity increased. Each night MiG-21s would stage out of Kep, Yen Bai, Phuc Yen and Quan Lang airfields.

Very little individual initiative was given to the MiG drivers. . . they were always closely directed by GCI radars. If an intercept were attempted by our fighters, the MiGs would land at the nearest field or run into China, where we could not follow.

The enemy cleverly attempted to entice our fighters to give chase on several occasions. As the MiGs flew south at supersonic speed, their GCI controllers would compute exactly when the intercept would be made by American fighters in the area. (The North Vietnamese knew the turning radius and missile systems capability of our aircraft). As we neared, the enemy fighters would turn and head north just out of missile-firing range.

Enemy GCI had direct liason with SAM and AAA under the fleeing MiG's flight path. As one of our fighters gave chase it would be lured over lethal anti-aircraft fire.

Communist pilots also entered an accelerated training program in 1971 and 1972. Before that time, a MiG driver trained in Russia, China or Czechoslovakia would fly perhaps 10 hours a month. Evidently the enemy recognized his lack of flying proficiency as we stepped up our action over the North.

MiGs were detected flying daily, training and patroling over the North, but again our hands were tied. No intercepts were sanctioned unless we were fired upon first or a threat to the fleet existed. During December 1971, B-52s conducting strikes in Laos and escorted by Air Force fighters were fired upon by two MiG-21s, staging out of Quan Lang. Flying at tree-top level to avoid radar detection, the enemy fighters were GCI-vectored behind the unsuspecting They made a supersonic pass, firing heat-seeking missiles, before the Air Force F-4s could react. Quickly they would disappear into the darkness below, diving to near ground level where they could not be picked up by the Phantom's radar system.

North Vietnamese MiGs made two more attempts to down a B-52 without success. It was only a matter of time until they scored, so a photo reconnaissance mission was ordered to overfly Quan Lang and establish the enemy's MiG strength.

An RA-5 photo bird was escorted by a large strike force of A-7s, A-6s, A-3s and F-4s to determine the enemy strength at Quang Lang airfield. The Vigie was fired on by AAA and the strike force promptly conducted an effective "protective reaction strike". Post-mission photos revealed MiG-21s being rolled into caves. Numerous SAM and gun emplacements ringed the field.

The field was repaired within a few days and the MiGs continued their harrassment of our operations as the North Vietnamese strengthened this field that posed the closest threat to the B-52s. A second recce flight was required to keep abreast of this build-up. Two attempts by other carriers to photograph Quan Lang failed, however, due to low visibility and cloud coverage.

On the 18th of January I was sitting in my rack when my squadron skipper, Commander Al Newman, got me on the phone. " "Duke, get your rear down to strike operations and prepare to escort a strike group over Quan Lang."

The news excited me. MiGs had been airborne on the previous strike, which left a slim possibility we might engage one, the very thing I had trained for. On our previous cruise we had flown intercept training hops in the Gulf. I always moaned and complained that I was not in a combat area to fly training missions, and that I would prefer not to be scheduled for them. Before I could settle into smug superiority, Rick Adams, a pilot for whom I have immense respect, grabbed me by the ears and retorted, "Listen, pukehead, every time you get airborne it's like buying a raffle ticket: the more tickets you buy, the better odds there are to win. The more you get airborne, the better chance of seeing a MiG." I listened... Rick was an ex-Blue Angel, combat veteran of '65, '66, '67, shot down twice over the North.

This Quan Lang MiG CAP would be like holding five tickets out of a hundred, so I was elated at the opportunity. I took out my rabbit's foot, rubbed it, then set out for the mission briefing. Crazy piece of fur and nails — I had carried it for the two years since a friend from the University of Missouri had given it to me. I rubbed it every mission, saying "this is the one I get a MiG." The guys in the squadron used to ask if the foot twitched when things looked promising.

The brief was lengthy. Instead of attacking from the Gulf side, we were going to attempt to surprise the enemy by flying south of the DMZ, then turning northward through Laos. The intent was to appear as a large force targeted in Laos.

Our formation of 35 aircraft got off without a hitch. If the enemy fired at the RA-5 there would be plenty of fireworks. Brian Grant, with Jerry Sullivan in his back seat, was my "wingie" again. Naturally I had the Irishman, Willie Driscoll, along for the ride. Norm McCoy, a MiG-21 killer in 1967*, led the second section of fighters.

No one broke radio silence as we went "feet dry". The countryside below passed in lush green. This was the first time any of us had flown this far north. We felt as if no other human had set sight on the jungle below.

"Hey, Duke, are you awake?" came the jovial Irishman's voice over the intercom. "Hey, Duke, is your rabbit's foot moving yet?" He always did something to break the tension or perk me up.

We continued north past the familiar mountain passes of Ban Nape, Mugia and Ban Kari, like a Sunday ride through Yosemite National Park, except these were easily identified by the barren bombed-out sandpits created by thousands of bombs delivered in attempts to slow supplies filtering south. Certainly strong evidence for man's inability to live without conflict. The further north we flew, the less destruction was visible.

Radio silence was finally broken as Commander Eggert called out Point Alpha, our first check point. All ordnance switches were armed.

Point Bravo was three minutes north. One-third of our force detached and 30 seconds later a second element split off toward the target. The tactic was to establish positions southwest and north of the field — if fired upon, we would attack the target simultaneously from three directions.

As "Point Bravo" was sounded over the radio my pulse rate

*McCoy was a VF-51 pilot who scored the 17th F-8 kill.

-38-

jumped: almost like being awakened from a long sleep with a bucket of cold water. I could see the A-7 bombers and the F-4 flak suppressors pull off to starboard, my cue to accelerate our section ahead of the second element. As I called for Brian to jam throttles to 100% I could see Quan Lang 20 miles away, nestled in a small valley in the middle of a large river bend. The mountains separating Laos and North Vietnam passed under my nose as the third element was called to turn inbound.

The ECM gear lit up — the Gomers knew we were in town. Fifteen miles out, Brian and I began to take 57mm fire. To avoid flying a predictable path, we jinked, turning and varying our altitude. Then the wonderful little black box that detects SAM radars operating flashed its warning. "Showtime, SAM low!" I blurted out. We were smack in the middle of two active SAM sites. (Showtime was VF-96's radio call.)

Roaring in over the field, we searched for MiGs taking off but the strip was empty. Brian and I had a fighter pilot's dream job: we were to overfly the field, check for MiGs, then fly north and place our section between Quan Lang and the enemy fields to the north, cutting off any attempt by the MiGs to reach the strike force.

The field was behind us in seconds. The northern SAM site had us locked up on radar; no time to think about twitching rabbits' feet. I was looking at the missile pad as two SAMs lifted... the dust and dirt flew up as the missile's booster propelled the telephone pole-like ordnance into the air. There is nothing, absolutely nothing, to describe what goes on inside a pilot's gut when he sees a SAM get airborne.

The booster dropped off, replaced by a white glow of flame accelerating the missile to Mach three-plus. I called Brian to turn hard port. As he did the SAM followed him, indicating it was tracking his aircraft, but he and Jerry hadn't seen the missile yet. As it closed rapidly I called for a break turn of maximum G — the SAM passed close to Brian's F-4, failing to detonate, possibly because we were inside minimum arm range. If it had gone off, Brian and Jerry would not be around, or they would have been eating pumpkin soup in Heartbreak Hotel shortly thereafter.

Our A-7 Corsairs were doing some good work on the field and the AAA sites. I heard Norm McCoy call out, "Let's hit the SAM site to the north." He and his wingman did just that with finesse. The attack birds were drawing most of the heavy flak as they rolled in on their targets.

Quickly the southern SAM site locked us up from two o'clock according to the warning gear — two more missiles were off the launchers in quick succesion. Breaking the other way, we came back over the field . . . as two SAMs were launched simultaneously from both sites! One was tracking me, duplicating my efforts to avoid it. This was gonna be rough. . . "Brian," I called up, "you're on your own!" We quickly got separated as they fired a total of 18 SAMs, in pairs, at us. MIGCAP was instantly a secondary mission as we concentrated on simple survival.

Waiting for the proper moment to begin my evasion tactic was agonizing. Panic rose up in my throat, urging loss of reason. At the last moment I pulled up with eight Gs after breaking down and starboard. The missile couldn't take the turn, going off a thousand feet below.

It was a mistake to pull so hard but it seemed the thing to do at the time, with telephone poles flying around in all directions. As I crawled through the air seeking that precious, lost commodity of airspeed, the north site fired two more SAMs! Brian saw them and maneuvered against the threat. The North Vietnamese were playing their cards right — we had made a terrible misjudgment by getting penned in between these two sites. The southern site caught us from the blind side and shot another missile at Irish and me — unbelievable!! Now I was too slow to do much even though Willie urged me to get out of the area in unrepeatable terms.

The tracking missile went off very close. No damage resulted. Wallowing around at 15,000 feet I pointed the nose straight down, selecting full afterburner, trying to gain back some of the energy I had lost in the SAM breaks.

Quick glances around revealed the attack birds pounding everything. The A-7s found the MiG storage areas hidden deep in the mountains south of the field. Norm and his wingman demolished the hated northern SAM site with Rockeye bomblets. A-6s were on the mark, cratering the runway with thousand-pounders. One A-7 driver made three passes through the maze of AAA attempting to drop ordnance that was hung up on his aircraft due to an electrical malfunction. These professional "earth movers" were sure earning their money — regardless of all the ribbing between the attack

This MiG-21, bearing 13 stars, was reputedly flown by the mysterious Colonel Tomb. But a fighter of this type was our first kill, shot down near Quan Lang.

"pukes" and the fighter "pukes", we respected each other utterly. The Vigilante was in the middle of it all, too, unarmed, killing 'em with film.

"Duke, look at that A-7, three o'clock," Willie called out. A SAM was chasing him downhill. At the last second he pulled up and the missile whistled by to plummet into the field's runway. Normally a SAM was set to explode any time it came within several feet of a solid object — thankfully most were not performing very well.

I noticed what I thought to be two A-7s exiting the target area to the north about four miles ahead. Looking back toward the field it struck me that something was unusual about these A-7s. Though they were too far away to identify, they had white glows near their tailpipes, indicating afterburning engines. Corsairs don't have afterburners.

"Irish, we have two bogies, low, heading north, but I can't tell what they are." I thought they were MiG-21s, but for two years I hadn't seen a MiG. . . and my rabbit's foot wasn't twitching. Two days before a pilot from VF-92 had called out, "MiGs, MiGs, MiGs!" when it was our own RA-5. The pilot had a hard time living it down. I wasn't about to make the same mistake.

Still nose-down, I accelerated to 650 knots and reversed, placing me in perfect position behind the unknown aircraft. As we closed I saw two of the prettiest delta-winged MiG-21s. The leader was about 500 feet off the ground in a canyon, with his wingman stepped up to his right at about 700 to 1,000 feet in fighting wing. "Showtime," I cried, "bandits, blue bandits (code for MiG-21), north of the field!" Brian heard the call and headed north after us.

Then something strange happened. I leaned back against my rabbit's foot. It dug into my flesh and I carry the mark from it today.

Willie and I were 200 feet above the ground doing 650 knots, looking up at the lead fighter. I went to boresight on the radar and called for Willie to do the same. "Duke, he's locked up on radar, in range! Shoot! Shoot! Shoot!" Just the situation to fire a radar-guided Sparrow, but my prior experience with this missile in training had not been good. In several of our practice engagements with drones I had fired Sparrows and missed while scoring hits consistently with Sidewinder.

I reached over, selected *Heat*, got a good aural tone (indicating the missile was sensing the heat of the enemy engine) and squeezed off a Sidewinder at dead six, calling "Fox Two!"

Just as the missile left the rail the MiG did what all MiGs do well —he executed a maximum G, tight turning, starboard break turn. He couldn't have seen me. Either his wingman called a break or his tail warning radar was working. I had an instantaneous plan view of him and he was really hauling, still in afterburner, at treetop level. His only defensive move would be either a nose-level or a nose-high turn.

I pulled up and rolled the F-4 port toward the MiG's belly side in a lag pursuit roll, placing us on the outside of the MiG's turn radius. With our superior speed we matched his turn rate. In the middle of the turn I looked back over my starboard wing to find the enemy wingman running away to leave his leader to fight me alone.

I could see my adversary's head thrashing around in the cockpit. He was not well trained, making the fatal mistake of dissipating all his energy in the break turn, and apparently he could not see me. His wings nearly clipped the rocks of the valley floor as our first 'Winder attempted to match his high G turn. The missile couldn't handle it, exploding out of lethal range.

Our Phantom was upside down 200 feet off the deck, doing 500 knots. "Blue Angels can fly inverted at these altitudes, but I'm no Blue Angel!" Panic rose up in my throat again as I thought we were going to crash. I jammed in full left aileron and full rudder while pushing forward on the stick. Instant negative G forced us into our straps and I ended up doing a fast aileron roll, which I had not planned, but we were right side up, pointing straight at the MiG with 40° to go to his heading.

His left wing started to drop as he reversed his turn. Irish was telling me to watch our altitude; no MiGs behind us. His voice quivered from the excitement, "Get 'em Duke." I knew that if I waited to fire another Sidewinder after the MiG's turn was completed, the missile could be defeated as the first was, so I squeezed the trigger and called, "Fox Two" at the moment he started his reversal.

The MiG was no more than 3,700 feet out in front of me and I was zero degrees angle off, a perfect envelope for the missile. Just as the enemy fighter's wings leveled, the Sidewinder hit him. The effect was spectacular as the whole tail came off and the remainder of the airplane went into a violent pitching, tumbling crash into the ground, creating a huge fireball. We passed through some of the debris as it scattered into a nearby village.

Brian, bless his faithful heart, had been clearing our six o'clock as well as he could, considering he was forced off our wing by four different SAMs while trying to catch up! He yelled, "You got him, Duke! Where is the other one?"

It was like a dream — none of this was really happening. Would I wake up only to find out it never happened? I experienced a momentary feeling of relief that the enemy was finally beaten. The excitement was beyond description — for the first time in 18 months a MiG had been sighted and destroyed by a fighter pilot of the United States. Irish was screaming in the back seat with exhilaration, but it wasn't over yet.

I picked up a silver glint at two o'clock. Brian saw him at the same time and called, "Duke, MiG-21 at two o'clock, three miles; I can barely see him." The enemy fighter was out of missile range. . . I lit the afterburners and accelerated to 650 knots but he was opening the gap by 50 knots. No MiG-21 Charlie could go that fast — this had to be one of the newer MiG-21Js with hydraulically boosted controls. The MiG-21 A, C and D models could never maintain that speed at sea level.

The 21 was so small that each time it ran straight away from us, we lost sight of it. Russian training was the only aid I had — Communist pilots were taught to turn from side to side in an attempt to clear their six o'clock. Each time he turned, we regained sight of his planform. The supersonic chase a hundred feet off the deck, weaving over trees, rocks and canyons was no picnic.

"Duke, what's our fuel state?"

"Willie, don't bother me now; I'm chasing a MiG," I snapped back.

"Duke! What's your state?" It was difficult to force myself to look into the cockpit . . . a quick glance away and the MiG could be gone forever. Thinking back on it, I would have probably chased him into China. I was astounded to find we had only 7500 pounds left — here was one case of an RIO most likely preventing the loss of an F-4 due to fuel starvation.

We started taking small-arms fire; tracers came up directly ahead. A slingshot could have brought us down at this altitude. As a last resort before breaking off I decided to fire a Sparrow. . . "I might get lucky or it might make him turn into me" were the only rationalizations I had. I went to radar boresight and squeezed the trigger. The EPU fired, but there was a short in the ejector cartridge — the missile failed to come off the rail.

"Red Crown, this is Showtime 112, three miles in trail of a blue bandit heading for Bai Thuong airfield." We were so low that the two Red Crown fighters in the Gulf just north of us failed to pick up my transmission, but our E-2 radar and radio relay aircraft gave them the message to vector our fighters in from the north. Nevertheless, the Gomer got through and flew into China. . . I wonder what he told his comrades when he got back.

The F-4 is highly maneuverable at speeds above 450 knots and I used every bit of her grace jinking back and forth, up and down, to deny the ground gunners a steady target. I knew from bird hunting that a darting duck, dove or quail was the hardest to hit.

Enough. . . I pulled back on the stick and looped toward Laos. Quan Lang came back in front of the nose with its familiar SAM sites. We had to press on through to get to the orbiting gas stations over Laos. The enemy locked on but we were well out of range.

We had enough fuel to make Da Nang, but we wanted to go all the way to *Connie*. The tanker we pulled up to had previously attempted to give gas to an A-7 without success but I wanted to try anyway. The fuel flowed like honey into our dry tanks.

Our beautiful *Connie* appeared off the nose. I wasted no time in calling up the Air Boss to request the traditional victory roll for splashing one bandit. The ship was running out of water in the small Gulf. . . "Negative, land immediately," came the terse reply.

"Negative, request victory roll."

"Negative! That's an order!"

"Yes, sir."

Irish and I came into the break smoking at 500 knots, below flight deck level. As we passed the ship I could see thousands of her men watching us from the catwalks. I made a six-G break turn, 90° angle of bank. . .

"Okay, Duke, let's don't blow it; now, take it easy," said Irish. He knew I was mad and no one could settle me down like Willie. We landed after one of my best passes of the cruise.

The flight deck was alive with men full of excitement and joy. Arms waving, victory fingers held high and a hastily scratched out flag: "Congratulations Lt. Driscoll, Lt. Cunningham."

As I shut down the engines and we raised canopies the deck flooded with men. I could see Admiral Cooper, Commander Task Force 77; Captain J.D. Ward, CO of the *Connie*; Commanders Al

Newman, my CO; and Dwight Timm, XO. The rest of VF-96 was crowding in behind them, and before anyone could say anything, Willie White, one of my favorite ordnancemen, nearly knocked over the captain, leaped up on the F-4 and shook my hand, "Mr. Cunningham, we got our MiG today, didn't we?" There were tears of excitement in his eyes, and rightfully so. He and thousands of other troopers had spent two years toiling in the heat, lifting Sparrows, Sidewinders and bombs aboard. Today *his* Sidewinder, *his* effort in making sure it was connected properly, *his* inspection of all the systems allowed that missile to perform effectively. . . just as the men working elsewhere on the ship, right down to the cooks and boiler tenders, made it possible for us to carry out our mission. Five thousand guys had just shot down a MiG-21 and they were proud of it.

Our Philippine cook, Ramerez, had a victory cake in the readyroom to celebrate more than a MiG kill — our tied hands had been freed to do the job right. Officers and men on the *Connie* were standing tall.

Radio Hanoi broadcast the following on 20 January 1972:

"U.S. pirates continue attacks against Indo-Chinese. The pirates were again punished and became crazy because of their bitter defeats of January 19, 1972. The U.S. imperialist aggressors recklessly sent many jet fighters to strike a populated area in Nehe An Province and incurred blood debts against our people, violating northern airspace. The pirates were appropriately punished by our armed forces and people. Two U.S. aircraft were blown to pieces right over the area upon which they had just dropped bombs to kill our compatriots. Many other aircraft were hit and fled. Following this attack the aggressors attacked many hospitals and schools, killing patients and students while wounding many others."

Eighteen SAMs and heavy flak were certainly in evidence, but only one A-7 was hit by a SAM and he made it back. Three SAM sites were destroyed, two AAA emplacements damaged, the runway bombed, the MiG storage cave demolished and one MiG-21 destroyed. I didn't see any hospital patients manning the weapons.

The next few hours after landing on *Connie* were full of questions and paper work, but I was still waiting to wake up from the dream. One of the pilots asked how it was up there and Willie replied, "Nothing like Belfast, Ireland!" Willie and I are both Irish Catholic.

The press came aboard and a trip to Saigon was arranged — I

This recon photo of Quan Lang Airfield was taken 19 January 1972, the day Willie and I bagged our MiG-21. The cloud at lower right is the exhaust of a SAM recently launched.

CAVE HANGAR

QUAN LANG AFLD

MSL LAUNCH EXHAUST

VN 447

RTE 7F

WIID

refused to talk to the news agencies and requested a cancellation of the trip. In the past reporters had loaded their interviews with questions such as, "Do you think this is a worthwhile war?" or "Do you want to be over here bombing Vietnam?" Quite often crews were misquoted, resulting in articles with a leftist anti-war slant. Straightforward interviews about what we were doing didn't sell newspapers. Let a pilot violate some rule or speak out against the war and one was sure to see him quoted.

One of our pilots was interviewed with questions such as, "Do you like flying in Vietnam?" The pilot replied, "Yes, I love flying. There are no FAA restrictions, there is excitement and this type flying is fun." The resulting article depicted the pilot as a man who loved bombing and killing Vietnamese for the thrill of it.

Another example: a news team was aboard filming scenes of carrier activity in the Gulf of Tonkin. During their stay Captain Ward gave *Connie's* war-weary men a stand-down day to let off steam. We had a steak fry on the flight deck complete with electric guitars and a rock festival. The fighter crews standing alert in their aircraft were served steak in the cockpit. The film team shot the whole thing, complete with sailors cutting up in grass skirts. The resulting TV special shown nationally back home presented our stand-down day as a typical day on the line during combat operations, indicating the "environment" we enjoyed in Southeast Asia.

The Navy stood behind my hesitancy to relate my feelings and experiences to the press, though later some fine interviews were given.

The commanding officers of all *Connie's* squadrons held a party to celebrate the first MiG kill in two years. Navy ships are dry, so we tipped our soda-pops and commenced celebrating. I felt on top of the world until someone asked, "Duke, what was it like to kill another human being?"

The words hit me full force, as if I were being knocked to the floor. I looked at my questioner, unable to reply. I turned and went straight to my room feeling as if the whole world had blown up. Always thinking of myself as a hard-core professional, I had believed that such a question would never faze me.

As I interrogated myself, a sickening feeling dug at my stomach. Dropping bombs for a year had not bothered me. Everything was so far removed when the 500-pounders went off in the jungle below, almost like bombing practice in the desert. But this was different. I observed another human being die because of me. I watched his twisted machine disintegrate, taking him to a horrible death, but at the time I guess my defense mechanisms allowed me to put it out of my mind.

Now, after the excitement had died down, I was confronted with it point-blank as I tried to make excuses for myself, saying it was in the line of duty. And I had a growing fear of relating my feelings to anyone, even to my best friends.

There was only one man on the ship I could turn to without fearing hints of combat ineffectiveness. As I knocked on the chaplain's door, thoughts of my parents' bringing me up in church flashed by. . . heck, as soon as I was away from home and on my own I stayed away from religion. Too late now. . . he opened the door and invited me in.

I wasted no time in telling him I had a personal problem that I wanted to talk over with him in the strictest confidence.

My mind was in turmoil as many questions poured out, questions that had to be answered, questions I had never let myself think about. When I left the chaplain I felt better, but the major doubts about God still gnawed at me.

The next day my CO called me to his room and confronted me with what I had told the chaplain, then put it to me straight: "Randy, how do you feel about combat flying now?" My first reaction was bitterness at the chaplain's violation of my trust and confidence in him. I could understand Commander Newman's concern, though —would I hesitate the next time I had a MiG locked into a fight? Before I left I had the basic problem worked through. I knew I would be able to do the same thing again, but I didn't have to like it — the act of killing someone was never a pleasant experience for me. The after-effects remain with me to this day.

Al Newman saw my despair, quickly ordering a few days in Cubi Point for Irish and me. The next morning we were off in the COD airmail S-2 with the good wishes of the flight deck crew. Airman Willie White wished us a good time in port, and guilt set in over leaving the rest of the guys to fight a war while I bathed in the sun. As we neared Olongapo City, though, a rest sounded pretty good.

Swooping down over Po City, I could see that the grapevine was working well. Word of the kill had preceded us, and there were several guys waiting at the field to greet the COD.

Congratulations began to pour in from everywhere as we settled in at Cubi, including, messages from Admiral Zumwalt, Admiral Moorer and, I think, every officer in the Navy. I wasn't allowed to call home and tell about the kill, so I sent a simple telegram, "Splash one blue bandit. I'm okay."

USS *Coral Sea* had just arrived at Cubi from the States with a mob of fighter pilots to crowd the club. The Navy fighter community is fairly small, so I was looking forward to seeing many of my old friends, especially Lieutenant Commander Jim "Ruff" Rulifson, my tactics instructor when I was a student in VF-121, an F-4 training squadron.

Ruff had tutored me as a pup, serving as an inspiration to many of us fledglings. He was another Jonathan Livingston Seagull. During those neophyte days I flew Ruff's wing with Lieutenant Jim Laing, one of the best RIOs around, in my back seat. Ruff had made it clear to me that he was going to get a MiG before I got my pants on, so my energetic attempt to find him at Cubi commenced at once.

I found him, alright, flat on his back in his room suffering from a severe headache — someone had forced too many Cubi specials down his throat at the club. My sympathies were with him, but there seemed only one way to get him back into the land of the living. I caught him square in the face with a glass of cold water.

Ruff hadn't changed a bit. He was as happy as I was about the kill, demanding to know every detail. Even with a student debriefing the instructor, Ruff's pure professionalism was in top form as he wanted to know how the F-4 and its weapons systems performed. Once again I could see why I studied so hard to be just like him. How lucky I had been to be with men like Commanders Dan Pederson, J.C. Smith, Roger Box; Lieutenant Commander John Nash; Lieutenants Mel Holmes, Peter Jago, Darrell Gary, Jerry Kinch, Jerry Sawatzky, Boots Boothby, Moody Suter, Roger Wells and so many others who had established a small cadre of men devoted to air-to-air tactics. Few people realize that air-to-air combat was deemed passe' at the time — the guns had been taken out of our aircraft in favor of missiles which we would launch at the enemy without hard maneuvering. In other words, dogfighting was to be a thing of the past. We knew better. These men were the Manfred von Richthofen, Oswald Boelcke, Erich Hartmann and Adolf Galland of the super-sonic era, and they had tutored each fledgling in preparation for our odyssey in Southeast Asia. From Fokker to Phantom the "Dicta of

Boelcke" still taught men how to kill and to survive in the air.

Ruff and I proceeded to the club. A real charger, the previous night's activities were not to stop him. We stopped by the swimming pool to find a bunch of attack pilots feeding monkeys by the galley. A commander threw out a piece of orange and the biggest monkey of the group, the undisputed leader, hissed loudly at the good commander, who returned and made a face at the monkey, mimicking an ape.

That proved to be a mistake. The monkey lit out after him, to the total surprise of the commander. The entire area broke into laughter as the six-foot two-inch, high-stepping naval officer was chased into the pool by a two-foot tall monkey. His pride tarnished and clothes dripping, the human retired quietly to his room.

I named the monkey "Che" after Che Guevara. Che became notorious for taking nothing from anyone and putting many a disbeliever in the pool. Something about that kind of spunk has to be right.

Ruff still looked pale, so we continued our journey to the Cubi Officers' Club. Most of the guys were in similar condition, so the club was virtually empty. It was great to sit down, order a big steak and just look at beautiful Subic Bay. Before I knew it, the sun was going down as the bar filled up and the song girl began singing the ever-popular "Yummy, Yummy, Yummy, I've Got Love in My Tummy."

We were greeted by Rear Admiral Ferris and Mrs. Cooper, wife of the Commander of Task Force 77. Admiral Ferris was elated that the two-year stalemate with the MiGs was broken, stating that *Coral Sea* would get the next one.

A friend, Lieutenant Garry Weigand, came over to the table and said, "Duke, you lucky S.O.B. You know how bad I want a MiG." I told him if he wanted one badly enough he'd get one. Just a few weeks later, on March 6, Garry shot down a MiG-17.

Looking at Ruff, I told the rest of the group that I would also get my second MiG before they got their first. I ended up in the pool in short order! Not the worst of punishments. I spent the next few days soaking up some rays beside the pool.

When *Coral Sea* set sail for the Gulf of Tonkin, I was virtually alone for two days to collect my thoughts. With all the activity of the past few days gone, all I could see was my own shipmates knocking heads with the North Vietnamese. . . and here I sat alone in my own little world.

The inactivity was more than I could stand. I walked down to the field to check on the next plane leaving for the ship. There wasn't one scheduled for three days, but I found out about a ride to Da Nang where I could hitch a helo to *Connie*. I left the next morning after a good night's sleep.

Arriving at Da Nang, I learned through the operations officer that I wouldn't be able to leave until two days at the earliest, so it was off to the officers' quarters on the Navy side of the base. My room consisted of 25,000 mosquitoes, a bad mattress and an ugly Vietnamese chow dog. There had to be a better place to stay somewhere, and the best place to find out was a local bar. Asking around for a bar, I got looked at as if I were crazy. Later I found out why.

Buried within Da Nang there was a bar called the Red Dog Saloon. Every Navy and Air Force pilot in Southeast Asia must have written his name upon its walls, and people were surprised that a military pilot was around who knew nothing about it. Directions as to its location were quickly given.

As I walked through the western-like doors, no one paid any special attention until an A-7 driver off *Connie* recognized me and shouted out, "Hey, MiG killer!" Another celebration party began immediately. Before long an Air Force jock came over and offered me a room on the Air Force side with its clean new buildings and good beds. After much merry-making, we staggered over to his squadron area.

The barracks were adjacent to the barbed wire perimeter with one South Vietnamese guard tower, but the Air Force honchos assured me all was safe. The Air Force captain who half-carried me over was Sammy White, another F-4 pilot. Once introduced, another celebration started as more Air Force pilots came over and invited me to meet their squadron skippers. Then more celebration parties. This was the first time I had ever sat down with Air Force pilots to collaborate about tactics, but I was in no shape to continue. . . and neither were they! About all I remember was waking up in a strange room with a terrible headache.

Looking over into the next bed, I saw the smiling face of Andy "Pig" Arnold. . . no question it was a set-up. Pig loved good food, and the Navy-side chow hall beat the Air Force by a country mile. Naturally I was in no position to duck inviting him over.

It takes team work to splash a MiG or win a trophy. The Admiral Joseph C. Clifton Trophy is presented annually to the Navy's outstanding fighter squadron, and VF-96 won it back-to-back in 1971 and 1972. Following our MiG-21 kill, the first in two years, the "Fighting Falcons" retained the Clifton Trophy. Here's Willie; our skipper, Commander Al Newman; myself, my wingman Brian Grant and his RIO, Jerry Sullivan

Four plates and six glasses of milk later, I had a profound appreciation of Andy's nickname. I had no doubt he could out-eat Paul Newman's 50 eggs, any day.

Andy and Sam turned out to be great friends, looking after my every need while I sojourned in Da Nang. Pig simply craved food, but Sammy was all questions, desiring to learn about the Navy's tactical doctrine. As I talked he even took notes! *This* was the kind of guy I would gladly fly combat with — enthusiastic, aggressive, willing to learn. After I returned Stateside, I received a treasured telegram: "Duke, splash one blue bandit, Sam." His energetic study bagged him a MiG-21 on August 19, 1972.

That night was almost a carbon copy of the previous evening's "engagement" with the Air Force, but there was no way I was going to let them put me away again. They had had too much fun doing it, and I'm sure if there had been a rocket attack, none of us would have known it. Still, enough went on to give me a sore head again, proving Air Force pilots don't drink warm milk and go to bed at 7 o'clock as I had once thought.

I slept most of the next day, since the weather was cooler than usual. I decided to take it easy that night since dinner was scheduled with the squadron commanders. Another fine evening. One of them asked how the Air Force could better its tactical program. With Pig and Sam smiling broadly, I told him point-blank to put Navy pilots in their planes. Sam, Pig and I thought it was really funny, but the colonel managed only a cracked smile.

He asked a second question: "How can our kill ratio be improved over 2:1 since the Navy's is 12:1?" I had one foot in already, so I put the other in by replying, "Colonel, the only way for the Air Force to better their kill ratio, is to start another war." Pig and Sam were nearly rolling off the table by now, and the colonel couldn't hold back anymore, laughing loudly as he said, "Okay, Cunningham, what will you have to drink?"

We had a gourmet's dinner and I retired early with a warm feeling about my new friendship with the guys in blue. Their hospitality was the best, with genuine welcome for me. On subsequent trips to the Air Force I received the same red carpet reception.

The next morning I was stuffed with mail bags into a chopper bound for *Connie*. The blue water below soon gave way to the white, churning wake of her props. . . and I could see F-4s launching, loaded with bombs. As we landed I was met by my skipper, "How do you feel, Duke?"

"Ready to fly, sir."

"Good. You take off in two hours and have the next alert watch."

Chapter 5

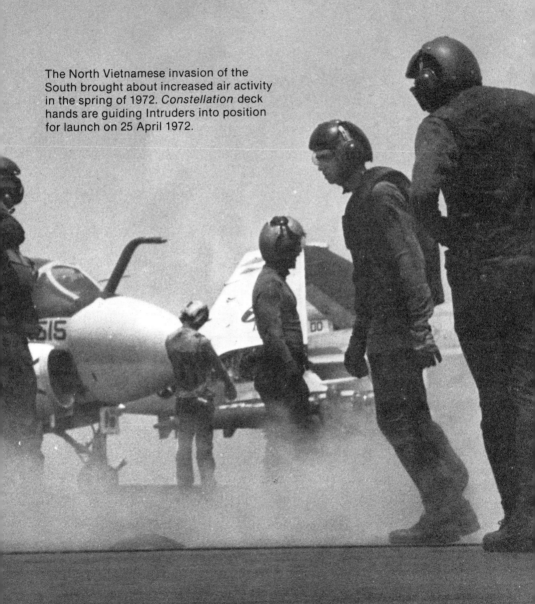

The North Vietnamese invasion of the South brought about increased air activity in the spring of 1972. *Constellation* deck hands are guiding Intruders into position for launch on 25 April 1972.

CHAPTER 5
NORTH VIETNAMESE INVASION

Uss *Constellation* was scheduled to sail for home during the latter part of March, 1972. After our last scheduled day in the Gulf of Tonkin, some of us flew into Da Nang in an attempt to catch a space-available hop to the States, rather than make the long crossing back with *Connie*.

The Da Nang flights were full, so we managed to get to Clark AFB only to wait two sleepless days and nights for a space-available flight. Finally, on March 22, I was on my way home with two combat tours under my belt — I would never have to see Vietnam again.

Landing in sunny San Diego on the 23rd, I picked up my family and drove straight to my home town, Shelbina, Missouri. A scant 12 hours after arriving, I received a call from my executive officer, who had made the flight back with us. "Randy, we have been ordered back to Vietnam. *Connie* has been recalled because of a major North Vietnamese offensive into the South."

Understandably, it was quite a blow to me, but it hit my parents harder. I thought Mom was going to call the Chief of Naval Operations at the Pentagon — she was flushed with anger. I drove my family back to San Diego, caught a 747 to Manila, and arrived shortly thereafter on board *Connie*. She was already conducting operations against the beseiged town of An Loc, 70 miles north of Saigon.

When the San Diego Chargers are losing six to nothing, and they have the ball, first down and goal to go on the one-yard line, they don't put in their scrubs. Neither did Hanoi, out for a military victory in the South and a political victory against the United States. The U.S. had been withdrawing troops with an anticipated 69,000 men leaving in May — Hanoi gambled on the lack of American will to wage war.

As pressure increased near the DMZ, *Connie* was moved north after defending An Loc. Then the dike really broke: 12,000 rounds of rocket, mortar and artillery fire slashed across the DMZ with 25,000 fresh North Vietnamese regulars equipped with Russian-built tanks and artillery to press Quang Tri, the South's provincial capitol.

Then Kentom, in the central highlands, was taken under seige. Sappers struck Cam Rahn Bay. An Loc was pressured by a fresh supply of troops and tanks, yet the South Vietnamese defenders held their battered positions. The Viet Cong were waging an effective multi-front campaign along with the regulars.

At Loc Ninh, a rural capitol north of Saigon, North Vietnamese troops crushed the South's defense system and routed the fleeing army. Things looked grim for the South as the North put most of its chips in the poker pot, drawing to an inside straight... while looking a full house in the face. NVN General Giap had 14 of his 15 divisions deployed across Indo-China, demanding maximum logistical support. This is precisely where President Nixon filled his full house.

Four aircraft carriers were in the Gulf, and *Midway* was en route. Our B-52 strength had doubled to 200 since 1971 while the insertion of Air Force F-111 and Navy A-6 aircraft could hold up supplies in the worst weather. Two more Phantom squadrons flew to Da Nang from bases in Okinawa and Korea. Our air power was effectively increased from 450 to 800 planes. The North Vietnamese invasion shattered President Johnson's 1968 agreement to stop bombing the North — a resumption of unconditional bombings was ordered.

Then our own politicians, Senator McGovern included, wanted to tie our hands as the North Vietnamese tried everything in the book to prevent us politically from stopping their embattled forces. The aircrews really got boiling mad. We sat on *Connie* and read about people like Ramsey Clark, a former Attorney General, visiting North Vietnam, along with actress Jane Fonda, claiming we were targeting the North's dike system. Miss Fonda was less than popular with us, and I'm glad she never came strolling over, especially after calling our returning POWs liars, concerning their stories of torture. I have no doubt that she placed many of our POWs in predicaments that led to torture as anti-war statements were forced out of them, then presented to anti-war activists.

Hanoi also cried out that we were bombing churches, hospitals and civilian areas. No doubt some civilian sections were accidentally hit, but what did they expect, as our aircraft bombed military targets while dodging AAA and SAMs? Accuracy isn't the greatest when jinking hard to avoid the black flak bursts. If a SAM chased a fighter-bomber with a full load, there was often no choice but to jettison the ordnance to avoid being killed by the missile. No telling where the bombs went.

The Gomers often placed anti-aircraft guns in the middle of large civilian settlements and on rooftops. If the guns weren't silenced, then the attack aircraft would be killed.

Hanoi was playing the extracted POW anti-war statements for all they were worth. Then staged films came out showing how well prisoners were being treated. Regardless of all the political pressure and dissent at home, Nixon had had enough. The man certainly had some problems, but we appreciated his direct, forceful dealings with the enemy. He was tired of watching us beaten up and thrown into a corner.

On March 30 at 2:00 am, hundreds of blips came to life on the Russian surveillance radars near Haiphong and Hanoi. Our A-6 drivers were the first aircraft over the North, flying at 50 feet to knock out the SAM sites that might affect the B-52s. Air Force F-105 Wild Weasels joined them with radar homing missiles.

Lieutenants Jim McKinney, Matt Connelly, Steve Queen, Dave Erickson, John Anderson and Greg Southgate flew MIGCAP to ward off a possible air attack, but a MiG would have been crazy to fly that night.

The intense action was incredible. . . over 200 SAMs were fired into the pitch-black night. Pilots said North Vietnam looked like it was on fire. Even though the Electric Whales (EA-3s) and EA-6s jammed enemy radar effectively, the attack pilots had a rough go of it down on the deck in the middle of it all. I know of one pilot who turned in his wings.

The linemen created a hole for our fullback — seventeen B-52s dropped 30 tons into the darkness over Haiphong. I could imagine the only thing visible of the Russian, Chinese and foreign ship crews in the harbor would be rear ends. The fuel farms and petroleum storage areas exploded, sending fireballs skyward, visible to the carrier crews 110 miles away.

By 0930 Hanoi was in panic. Loudspeakers blared warnings and civil defense instructions as thirty-two Air Force F-4s attacked warehouses and any petroleum storage areas that remained on the city's outskirts. Evacuation orders spread through the populace.

To a small group within Hanoi the holocaust was music — the POWs were overjoyed at the American show of strength. Their supposedly fearless guards quivered and dived under anything available. One guard was seen to curl up in a tight ball in a corner crying, "Don't kill me!" During the bombings in December, some of the guys were able to sabotage enemy equipment; as the B-52s hit, Lieutenant Steve Rudluff, USN, reportedly poured dirt and urine in the gas tanks and oil cases of five trucks.

At 1430 Sunday, 40 Navy jets launched against heavily defended Haiphong to hit truck parks, SAM sites, AAA sites, storage areas and other military targets. Lieutenant Dave Lichterman rolled in on Kien An airfield, dropped Rockeye bombs and watched the MiGs parked in revetments go up in flames. When Dave returned, his linecrew painted the traditional MiG silhouettes on the side of his A-7 — the only difference being that starting carts were hooked up to the MiGs, representing ground kills.

As the day neared its end, 250 SAMs had been launched at the strike forces. Our electronic jammers had sure done their job, though — only two of our aircraft were hit, not the 15 claimed destroyed by Radio Hanoi. Only four MiGs got airborne, three of which were shot down.

VF-96 was in on it, too. Brian and I struck Happy Valley south of Haiphong, the entry point to the mountain passes leading into Laos. Our 40-plane strike group met surprisingly light opposition. The A-6s and A-7s went after the rail yard and storage areas while my F-4 section went after the flak emplacements with Rockeyes. Whenever the enemy's guns opened up on the rest of the force, Brian and I would destroy the guns.

Flak suppression is normally a rough mission, but to our surprise, the AAA was light. Irish noted all the empty gun emplacements left over from the 1965-67 period when Happy Valley was one of the hottest areas in Vietnam. Evidently the North did not think we would resume the bombings, as I mentioned earlier, moving most of their guns into Laos, South Vietnam and Cambodia. Our strike was almost uneventful except for a few SAMs and light AAA. One village housing two 23mm and four 57mm gun emplacements was destroyed.

Prior to our coming back aboard *Connie*, a second strike group had launched, leaving the decks clear for the enlisted crews to rearm our aircraft. As soon as we trapped, it was off to strike operations for the debrief, then prepare for the next strike, only two hours away. Surprisingly, no one appeared fatigued... It could have been the excitement, or the will to deliver the enemy a taste of his own medicine before the politicians forced a halt which would allow the North to regain strength. If that happened again, it was a sure-fire ticket to death or the Hanoi Hilton, for some of our pilots that would not go otherwise. The adrenalin was pumping hard enough to keep us airborne, regardless of the reasons — we wanted to get back out to the action.

Ramerez, a cook to put the Brown Derby to shame, was waiting for us with huge double egg, double fry, double cheeseburgers. Irish always had a big appetite, but after each mission he ate like it was the last supper.

The rules of engagement were reviewed carefully so that each crew knew what could and could not be done over North Vietnam. Any variance from selected and approved targets could mean a long stay in Leavenworth. We could react to any gun or missile site firing at us or at downed crews and, we could go after MiGs; otherwise, stay with assigned targets.

This time I got into the center of the action over Haiphong. We were to hit a supply storage area where Russian ships had unloaded war materials. We were strictly forbidden to bomb any foreign vessel, but intelligence indicated the ships had departed. Each of us had to memorize the target location hidden among the thousands of tributaries and finger-like coves that make up Haiphong harbor. AAA was thick in the harbor, making identification that much more difficult if one were not thoroughly familiar with the target area.

One by one our 40-plane strike group rendezvoused over the ship, jockeying for position in the formation. Gomer radar had us from this point on. The F-4s took on extra gas to give effective MiGCAP to the strike birds.

Our target was within range of six MiG bases, but the North Vietnamese were leaving the gray Navy airplanes alone. Hanoi relied on its air defense network to take care of the eastern side of the

Phantoms, Vigies and Corsairs are arranged on *Connie's* stern preparing for launch over North Vietnam. My regularly assigned aircraft, number 110, is visible in this shot.

city — the MiGs were to stop the waves of USAF bombers. In 1972 the Air Force had a kill ratio against the MiGs of 2:1, whereas the Navy accounted for 12 MiGs for each loss. Back in 1968 the Navy had grasped the seriousness of its lack of air combat training through the Ault Report, resulting in better-trained crews in 1972. The USAF was slower in coming to this realization.

The Gomers supposedly had a sign at Phuc Yen airfield: "Rule One — don't eat yellow snow. Rule two — don't attack gray Phantoms."

As our force moved up the coast line just out of SAM range, the ECM strobes started ticking off enemy radar tracking. Six SAMs were fired out of range, exploding several miles away. The Red River Valley lay south, glimmering in the sun's reflection.

We were covering the strike birds both with air-to-air missiles and Rockeye bombs. Amazing weapon, the Rockeye — it broke in half at altitude to disperse hundreds of tiny bomb-like darts capable of penetrating tank armor or fragmenting against soft targets. The Rockeye could cover an entire gun emplacement, preventing the site from concentrating fire on the strike aircraft.

The air-to-air mission entailed our watching the sky full of twisting aircraft, identifying each one as it raced by at supersonic speeds, lest it prove to be a MiG.

"May Day, May Day!" broke out over the radio. An A-7 not far off the beach was hit and going down, the enemy gunners following him. The pilot ejected and that beautiful parachute popped open, but the gunners kept firing at him as he floated down. A quick switch to the SAR frequency. . . we heard the pilot say he was alright, but he would appreciate our getting him the hell out of there as quickly as possible.

The entire mission diverted, as had happened before on so many occasions, to insure no NVA got to the downed pilot. I had a chance to look around — roaring oil fires could be seen for 50 miles; the harbor itself seemed to be on fire. I could see the pilot's buddies circling him, but most of them had already dropped their ordnance. I remember thinking, "That poor S.O.B." as the A-7 pilots had to depart, due to low fuel states. The downed pilot called, "Thanks, guys. Can't you stay a bit longer?" I came up on the radio, almost angry, "Blue One, we have you in sight and will kill anything that gets close to you!" He liked that.

A close-up of "Showtime 110," the plane I normally flew with Willie, being prepared for catapulting. A carrier flight deck is a noisy, crowded, dangerous place, and the men who work there are paid only a fraction of their worth.

Two Russian freighters entered the area, heading straight for our man. I told Brian to arm his bombs and take a one-mile trail position. Irish was busy checking our six o'clock since MiGs loved to sneak in on slow-flying SAR birds. If the Russian fired on us, which we deeply hoped for, then Brian would blow them out of the water.

Before leaving the area, one of our A-7s flashed in front of us and placed a few 20mm rounds in front of the first freighter. It kept coming. . . so did I, letting down to 200 feet, jinking back and forth just in case the ship opened fire. I could see the Russians on the deck as we neared. There would be no "accidental" running down of one of our pilots today. The Ruskies got the message and turned away from the pilot in his raft. As we pitched up, I could see one of our helos over the pilot, totally vulnerable now to guns firing from the beach.

I lined up on the tracers and pressed in for the kill. The Gomers saw us coming, switching their fire to my Phantom. Tracers came flying past the canopy. Brian was one mile ahead of us, attacking another gun.

"Duke, SAM at two o'clock!" Irish blurted out. The missile failed to track, exploding high above. Looking back toward my target, I placed the gun sight right on the muzzle flashes and released the bombs. Black bursts from another gun exploded at our three o'clock — I broke port, then back to starboard toward the Gulf. Out of the corner of my eye I could see Brian pulling off target as his bombs sailed down for a direct hit.

Brian was jinking so hard it was difficult to tell which way he was going to turn. . . "Brian," I called, "come hard starboard so we can catch you. We are one mile in trail and closing." We rendezvoused and checked each other for hits. It looked like a clean bill of health. Sea Cow looked over at us, shaking his head as he said, "Who needs it!"

The helo had made it with the uninjured pilot out into the Gulf. My rabbit's foot was still intact and Irish sang with joy. Our pilots went through this type of fire every day. We knew the Russian and Chinese freighters were bringing in the North's supplies. Is it any wonder we were happy when President Nixon made the decision to mine the harbors? Is it any wonder we hated the names of Jane Fonda and Ramsey Clark and wondered why Senators Proxmire and McGovern had deserted us?

We came aboard *Connie* with enough time to debrief the mission and assume the "alert five", a watch we sat in our Phantoms, hooked up to catapults — we could launch in less than five minutes if necessary. After the watch we had about four hours to sleep, but it was difficult to turn off my mind — two or three more missions were on for the next day.

For the next four weeks we hit the North hard. The carriers *Midway* and *Saratoga* joined *Coral Sea*, *Hancock*, *Kitty Hawk* and *Constellation* in the Gulf. Sixteen attack aircraft and 21 helos were downed with the loss of many aircrews killed, POW or MIA. But the North Vietnamese invasion was stifled.

A story made the rounds of one North Vietnamese soldier who had walked into Da Nang one afternoon and surrendered. When asked why he had given up, he related the story of thousands of his comrades having been killed during the unexpected heavy bombings. At the last he had been ordered to carry two large rockets down the Ho Chi Minh Trail. He had been shot at, bombed and almost killed. Upon arriving near the outskirts of Da Nang he reported to a V.C. lieutenant, handing over the rockets. The lieutenant placed the two missiles in launchers and fired them toward Da Nang as the soldier watched. Then the officer walked over to the soldier, said "Good job. Now go get two more rockets." The soldier said B.S. and turned himself in. The story was true, as far as any of us could tell.

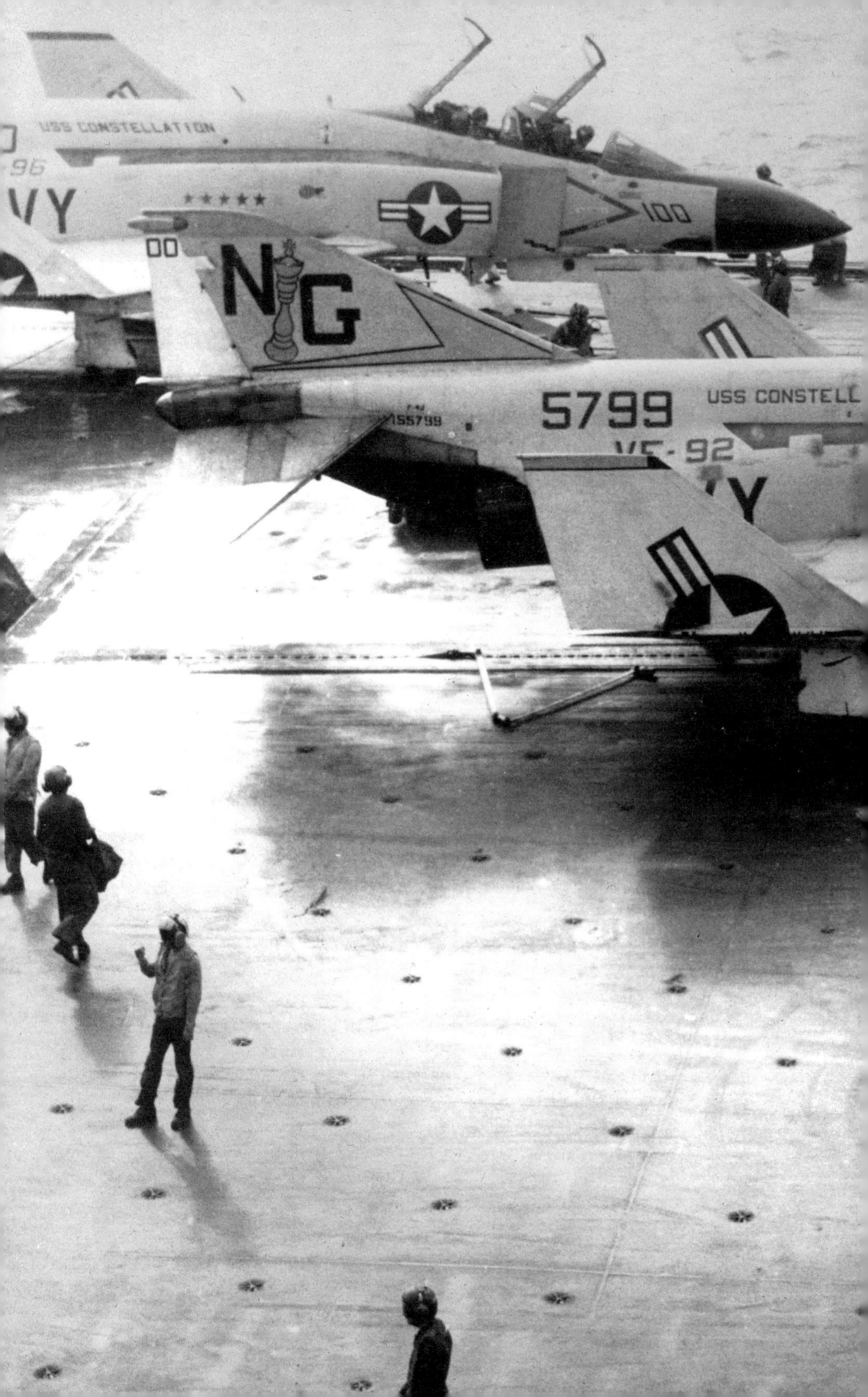
USS CONSTELLATION
100
00
NG
5799
USS CONSTELL
VF-92

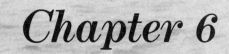

Air Wing Nine was one of the few units in which both fighter squadrons were MiG-killers on the same cruise. Here's "Showtime 100" and "Silver Kite 200," the CAG-birds for VF-96 and VF-92, respectively, during May 1972.

CHAPTER 6
MIG MASTERS

Even though my January 19 MiG kill stirred up hopes for frequent engagements, getting at the tiny Russian-built fighters was not an easy task. The Air Force got MiG-21s on February 21 and March 1 (the first USAF victories since February, 1968). Then Garry Weigand and his RIO Bill Freckleton of VF-111 off *Coral Sea* shot down a MiG-17 on March 6.

It was quite a fight. Garry flew wing on Jim Stillinger to provide FORCECAP on an RA-5 photo mission over Quan Lang airfield. The Vigilante pilot saw two MiG-21s pass in front of him, heading for the strike group, then Commander Tooter Teague and his wingman, Dave Palmer, found a gaggle of MiG-17s. During the tangle, Sidewinders and Atolls (Soviet-built version of the Sidewinder) were fired, but no one was hit as both sides retired.

Garry and Jim orbited above "Red Crown", USS *Chicago*, in Brandon Bay, listening to the action. Then they were vectored into North Vietnam to set up a CAP station 50 miles north of Quan Lang in case the MiGs decided to make their retreat in that direction.

The Navy's ace controller, Chief Nowell, picked up bogies on his scope buried within the bowels of *Chicago*. Finally a bandit call came and the Phantoms were vectored in. At a scant two miles separation, the F-4 crews could not pick up the bandit. Stillinger called out, "No joy; bogie dope!" meaning no visual contact, keep information coming. Chief Nowell responded with, "Look low!" As the ank they saw a MiG-17 pulling up its nose to engage.

Jim maneuvered in behind the MiG, but the Gomer saw him and broke into the F-4, forcing an overshoot and high yo-yo. Garry went high to cover the action, as the MiG driver turned back into the attacking F-4. Stillinger made four passes on the maneuverable

MiG and each time he was met and countered. Jim got off a 'Winder, but the wiley 17 pulled a high-G turn, to defeat it.

With the fight going nowhere, Jim called, "I can't stay behind him. I'm going to unload and run. Do you have me in sight?" Garry rogered as he rolled in on the MiG. As Jim pushed the stick forward to zero G and lit the burners to run, the MiG went after the F-4. Garry rolled down into the 17's blind six o'clock and fired a Sidewinder. The missile went straight into the enemy tailpipe, blowing the tail off the aircraft.

That evening I received a message one would expect from a great fighter pilot: "Duke, I got mine today and I'll get a second before you do." I wish he had found another MiG in short order, but two full months elapsed before the Navy shot down any more MiGs, although the Air Force got four more 21s by the end of April.

On May 6 things really busted loose. The Navy scheduled major strikes on Haiphong, Vinh and Bai Thuong. Intelligence reported on the night of May 5th that there could be as many as 14 MiGs at the latter field.

Lieutenant Commander Jerry "Devil" Houston and his RIO, Lieutenant Kevin Moore, were a part of the TARCAP, the close escort for the strike force, from VF-51 off *Coral Sea*. When the A-6s arrived over Bai Thuong, they immediately began calling, "MiGs everywhere, MiGs, MiGs, MiGs." It sounded good to Jerry, but the TARCAP was assigned to the F-4 bombers and the A-7s 15 miles south of the action. The strike force accelerated into the area. Then the lead F-4 bombers began calling MiGs everywhere! Jerry couldn't stand it any more, so he pushed up the throttles and began to descend to gain speed. Sailing into the area, Kevin told Jerry, "There're your A-6s. . . one. . . two. . .three. . . and there're your MiGs!"

Jerry latched onto a MiG-17 that was pumping its cannon away at three A-6s. Calling for the A-6s to break, Jerry lined up dead six on the MiG, but the lead A-6 would not break. It turned out to be the CAG dragging the MiG out away from the other attack birds. Devil had a good Sidewinder tone, but both the MiG and the Intruder were lined up for a perfect shot — which jet's heat was the missile sensing? Nearing minimum range, Jerry decided to shoot. . . and nothing happened! As he rechecked all the switches, the 'Winder came off the rail and went straight down! Then straight up! As

Houston and Moore flew through the hump-backed smoke trail of the missile, it straightened out and headed for the MiG.

CAG saw the missile and broke — he knew that a MiG-17 going 500 knots had very poor control response. Sure enough, the MiG could not match the turn and the Sidewinder flew into the engine, taking the jet apart.

With the presence of MiGs definitely established in the Bai Thuong area, it was decided to launch another strike at the airfield the same evening. VF-114 provided the MIGCAP, launching from *Kitty Hawk* at 1630. Pressed for time, the four Phantoms did not get to refuel before being vectored by Red Crown: "Bogies, bearing 330° at 40 miles." Lieutenant (jg) Joe Cruz, in the back seat of Lieutenant Bob Hughes' F-4, got a pulse Doppler contact on his radar, so Hughes assumed the lead for the pursuit with responsibility for the Visual Identification Pass.

Lieutenant Commander Pete Pettigrew and Lieutenant (jg) Mike McCabe fell into the wing position to follow Hughes in. Pete was one of the finest aviators in the Navy, and a great guy to have for a "wingie." At 15 miles the Phantoms went to afterburner and at four miles the controller called, "Check left at ten o'clock." Everyone had an immediate tally-ho on four MiG-21s, easy to spot against the haze layer. The 21s were at 4,000 feet, the Phantoms at 5,000. In trail with wingmen tucked in tight, the enemy pilots apparently could not see the approaching American fighters.

Pettigrew called for McCabe to watch the lead section while he kept his attention on the trail formation. Then Pete radioed Hughes, "You're shooter, I'm cover... let's engage!" A mile out the MiGs saw the two Phantoms, turning into them. Hughes fired a quick Sidewinder with serious doubts about its guiding, but the missile turned sharply and guided toward the trailing MiG. Amazingly it blew up, taking sections of the MiG's wings and tail off and opening a large hole in the fuselage. Trailing smoke, the MiG went down and crashed into the ground.

Hughes turned hard to line up the lead MiG, firing two more Sidewinders — they failed to guide, going ballistic. As McCabe kept an eye on the other two MiGs, Pettigrew went after the elusive quarry, pulling hard to the inside of its turn. Putting his nose on the MiG, he got a good tone and fired, just as Hughes' 'Winder exploded near the MiG and Pettigrew's missile flew up its tailpipe. Pete watched the 21's cockpit section come tumbling out of the resulting fireball after pitching right, then coming back left. Then the MiG's canopy came flying off, followed by the enemy pilot! The parachute opened as Pettigrew roared by less than 200 feet away.

The other two MiGs were still no threat, but it was time to leave. Pete and Bob executed a hard nose-down turn into the 21s, lit the burners and blasted by the enemy aircraft, which could not get turned around in time to pursue the Phantoms, already five miles away. The entire engagement had lasted but a minute and a half.

With three MiG kills in one day, everyone was looking for more bandits on May 7th, but there were no takers and strike operations went uncontested. A few of us aboard *Connie* found an excuse for a party that day when we learned the next day's mission would be a MiGCAP in the middle of all the "fun." Sea Cow was the first with the news — together we charged in on the never-ending cribbage game that Brian and Jim "Foxy" Fox played in the former's room. Brian was letting out a string of profanity as we knocked on the door — Foxy had just beaten him. What a riot to see Brian open the door in his skivvies, with the red glare of defeat on his face! Foxy was roaring with laughter; Brian broke out in a wide grin — these guys were fanatics on the game, playing almost nonstop when given the chance.

Steve Shoemaker and Steve Queen, next door to Brian, came over to see what all the commotion was about. Shoemaker loves good-looking women, Scotch, beer and popcorn (or papa charlie, as the Shoeman calls it). Since the former choices were out, Queenie brought over his papa charlie maker. We were also out of ice. Being bold, and a bit stir-crazy, we launched a top secret mission to the captain's personal ice locker with great success. Captain Ward probably still wonders where his ice went on May 7, 1972.

With Queenie and Shoe back with the prize, Brian's room was full. We had a great time, topping the evening off by catching the scheduled movie, "The Green Berets" with Duke Wayne. No question we were avoiding deep thought over the next day's mission. Sure, we wanted to get MiGs, but we had been in the Gulf of Tonkin for a long time, and on borrowed time at that, since we had been called back for extra duty. We had lost some fine friends, and a month of 18 to 20-hour days, getting shot at in the process, was enough to split anyone's nerves. Stealing the captain's ice and other such nonsense helped us keep our sanity. We knew we weren't invincible — just the previous April 27 a Navy F-4B had been shot down by a MiG-21 with Atoll missiles.

Mission planning was thorough — Brian and I would be in the MiGCAP preceeding a 35-plane strike force targeted on the enemy's driver-training school and its 300 to 400 trucks. And *Connie's* force would be but the second element in a multi-carrier assault against the enemy's already tattered logistical system. Irish and I, Brian and Sea Cow, could be in the middle of North Vietnam within easy reach of most of the major MiG fields.

Our cat shots, rendezvous and weapons checkout went smoothly, but the weather was scattered to overcast. As we neared the coast I could make out the heavily defended Red River Valley with its tributaries leading into the hourglass rivers. All set to go, we could not get approval from Red Crown to enter the North. Repeated attempts to get the okay failed, making me fidgety: "Red Crown, Showtime 112. We're either going in or cancelling." A voice crackled back into my helmet, "Go get 'em, tiger. You are cleared to the North."

With Brian in perfect position we headed northwest to pass just south of Ninh Binh, ECM gear flashing. Two SAMs came out of the center of the hourglass, but they weren't tracking as they soared above us. Approaching Che Ne up the karst ridges, I decided to swing into the valley and take a look for MiGs that might be coming down from Dong Suong, Ho Lac or Gia Lam. What a mistake that was! No sooner were our noses stuck into the valley than SAMs and 85mm opened up. With a quick port turn we were back over the safety of the mountains.

Red Crown called with "unknown bandits, 340° and 60 miles" out of Yen Bai. I saw Irish give me a thumbs-up in the mirror and we turned for the intercept. Ordnance switches were armed and ready to go. Fuel tank jettison was ready to get rid of that big tank with its extra weight and drag. Then Red Crown lost contact with the bandits... the MiGs must have slipped below the mountain ridges to avoid detection.

A flash caught my eye! My heart fell into my stomach as I saw six grey forms at two o'clock low coming up out of the clouds. My stomach settled as I recognized A-7s from the previous strike group. As they flashed by, Irish picked up two radar contacts at ten o'clock

On 8 May, almost four months after our first kill, Willie and I got a second MiG. Though my expression conceals it, I enjoyed telling the troops about the 17 we bagged south of Hanoi.

closing at 1,000 knots.

Frustration. . . there was no telling where they were. Two of *Kitty Hawk's* fighters were making a sweep somewhere out there and the Air Force had fighters just north of us striking Yen Bai. We were obliged to see the bogey aircraft before shooting, virtually eliminating the head-on potential of the Sparrow missile system. The Sparrow had been designed for "blind" shooting by men who thought the day of dogfighting was gone.

When all the statistics were in after the war, the missile was found to be defective most of the time, or just plain useless.

By now our strike force was over the target with us ten miles north. For all I knew, they might be flying right into a nest of MiGs, so I called for a 180° turn to give cover for the force. Just as we got turned around Red Crown called, "Bandits closing at your six o'clock and 20 miles." We turned around again and headed west.

From 10,000 feet the haze layer obscured the ground below. . . and any MiG lurking there. Red Crown made a call but my radio garbled it: Irish couldn't understand what was said, either. I started to call Brian to get the dope when he called out, "Duke, in place, port. . . go!" He was bound to know something I didn't, so I began the left turn, placing my F-4 in trail after 90° of turn to check Brian's six o'clock. We'd lost a couple of fighters earlier when the lead aircraft could not check his wingman's tail.

As I called Brian's six clear, I selected full afterburner, then pulled hard up and to the inside of the turn to place myself abeam of Brian at one mile — now we could clear each other's tails. No sooner had I taken a look behind my buddy than a MiG-17 came screaming up through the haze layer in afterburner, shooting at Brian!

The MiG's 23mm BBs were falling short. "Brian, MiG-17 at your seven o'clock!"

"WHAT?"

"You've got a 17 on your tail and he's shooting! Get rid of your centerline, unload and outrun him!"

Brian punched off the big tank and started to extend away from the MiG. Now within gun range, this MiG driver must have come in last in his gunnery class — he just wasn't pulling enough lead.

"Brian, I'm high at your nine o'clock. . . don't push negative Gs or you'll fly through his BBs."

Our intelligence boys, bless them, had told us the 17 was not carrying Atoll missiles — all we had to do was to get out of gun range. When Brian had opened the gap to around 3,500 feet I saw a missile blast out from under the enemy fighter!

"Brian, Atoll. . . break port!" The F-4 hauled around in a tight six-G turn and the missile, though it tried, just couldn't make the corner, and the break enabled the nimble 17 to cut across the circle to get back in gun range.

"Brian, he's closing again. . . unload and go again!" The MiG was shooting but he couldn't get the proper lead. . . and I was about 60° off the MiG's tail, so I couldn't get a Sidewinder shot.

As Brian pulled away Willie called, "Duke, look up! Two MiG-17s meeting us head-on." As I looked up I saw the MiGs pass 200 feet over my canopy. "Irish, you watch 'em. By the time they get turned around, they'll be out of the fight." I was about to get my first lesson in the turning ability of the MiG-17.

My concentration was bore-sighted on the fighter chasing Brian and Sea Cow —their F-4 had reached the same position ahead of the MiG as before and I was afraid the Gomer was going to shoot another Atoll. I still had 60° off the MiG's tail —no 'Winder could hack a shot now, but I fired anyway. The missile tracked and strained for its quarry, finally giving up to fall below, but it sure scared the MiG driver, who made a hard break into it. . . getting him off Brian's tail! He reversed right in front of me and started to run. This was too good to be true — surely he knew I could catch him. Yeah, he did. . .

"Duke, MiGs at five and seven shooting!" came Willie's strained voice.

"Impossible," I thought. "No plane can turn around that fast." Irish later told me that the 17s were 4,000 feet apart when they passed over. They turned in toward each other and completed 180° turns *without crossing* each other's flight path! Yep, impossible, but there they were firing away at us.

I had a tone on the fleeing MiG, so I squeezed the trigger — it was a classic shot. The missile came off the rail, did a little wiggle, and flew right into him. The fighter crashed into the mountain it had been heading for. But it could still be an effective sacrifice play for the enemy.

With Brian sitting up high over me I called, "Alright, Brian, I'm going to pull hard down into your port turn and drag the MiGs out in front of you . . . shoot them off my tail!" It was my turn in the barrel and I was anything but calm, cool and collected. The cannon shells flashing past my canopy unnerved me — the 23mm twinkles out of the wing roots, but that 37mm puts out a BB the size of a grapefruit. Its muzzle flash looked a good five feet long. As I went port, the MiG at seven o'clock closed in, sending grapefruits over my head in larger numbers. "Well, that's not going to work!" bounced through my mind as I turned to look the enemy pilot in the face — I could see the little Gomer inside with his beady little Gomer eyes, Gomer hat, Gomer goggles and Gomer scarf.

I reversed and tracers began zooming by the right side of my canopy! "Brian, get in here! I'm in deep trouble!" I tried one more reversal but Hanoi Charlie was still there, blasting away. Training adages began bouncing through my mind: "Never turn into a MiG-17." Yeah, definitely the right advice, but I couldn't go up and deplete any more airspeed since this would give the slower MiGs even more of an advantage.

I rolled my beautifully-constructed McDonnell product into a 120° nose-low slicing turn, burying the stick in my lap. I put a good 12Gs on the aircraft, tearing wing panels, popping rivets, and breaking a flap hinge. All that stuff we had pumped into our brains about the classic air battles of the past flashed through my mind. Virtually nothing is new in air fighting, only realigned or modified according to scenario. One didn't break into a MiG-17, just as a P-51 or P-38 didn't make a habit of turning with the Japanese Zero for any length of time. The MiG turned inside of me and I looked out of my canopy to see him a scant ten feet away! I could read his side number and count rivets. . . and he still had two missiles slung under his wings.

I called for Brian to pitch up into the vertical. He was at my one o'clock and I wanted to pull to the inside of his port turn. If the MiGs followed me, Brian could roll over the top and get a shot. Hanoi Charlie and his Gomer buddy weren't buying the goods — they started pressing me again.

"Brian, I'm diving for the clouds." Full forward stick and I was in the milky deck. . . with the MiGs right behind me. Up to this point I hadn't used afterburner because I was afraid of the remaining Atolls. Two J-79s at full cooker would have presented a great heat source. As soon as I got into the clouds I went into full burner and accelerated out to 550 knots real quick.

Brian radioed that he couldn't see all of us. "That's good — they

North Vietnamese MiG-21 pilots briefing in front of their aircraft. Their Soviet-made flight gear contrasts with the leather jackets and helmets frequently worn by MiG-17 drivers.

can't see me, either," I thought. "Brian, I've got 550 knots coming out toward the sun." If the MiGs did fire a heat-seeker, it would most likely select the sun's heat and not my tailpipes. And hopefully they would be blinded by the sun, if nothing else.

As I popped up, Brian let out a "Tally Ho!" And there he was, high at my five o'clock, in perfect position to jump the MiGs if they came out after me. Sure enough, they popped out right behind me, and Brian rolled in on them. The two MiGs wanted no part of Brian, diving back into the sanctuary of the overcast. As I reversed, Brian and I got into position and became the hunters. We went back into the clouds, but there was no way to spot the 17s.

Red Crown came back on frequency and announced MiGs staging out of Gia Lam, Hanoi's main field. Since we still had plenty of fuel, we patrolled the area with no results. All our attack aircraft had exited safely and other Phantoms had launched to cover our withdrawal in case the MiGs tried to jump us.

As we were on the way out I spotted a line of trucks about five miles long. The air-to-air fighting was certainly over now, so I rolled in on one of the trucks. Brian asked what in the world I was doing —we only had air-to-air missiles, no bombs. I figured that a truck might provide enough of a heat source for a Sidewinder, so I was trying to get a tone on one of them. I had tried it once before, with no success, but the guy I picked on this time must have needed a valve job — I got a good tone and squeezed off the missile. It slammed into the truck, dead center, sending a fireball into the sky.

Red Crown was on the ball, vectoring us to the spot where we had entered the North earlier. And there was one of *Kitty Hawk's* A-6 tankers with his refueling hose already extended.

Returning to the ship was another jumble of thoughts. I was happy to have downed my second MiG. . . even happier to be alive. Getting over the intense fear of being shot at was like being born again. To come so close to death with every sense activated, heart pumping, nerves keyed up, muscles tense, the mind forced to react like a high-speed computer. . . when it was over, a strange euphoria set in. In the midst of it all, I still had the sense that I was only the extension of the 17- and 18-year olds on *Connie* who made up the flight deck crew, the technicians, the mechanics and all the others.

As *Connie* came into sight a short distance off the coast, my first impulse was to request a victory roll for the troops to make up for being denied the last one. Irish switched up to tower frequency, "Sir, request victory roll for splashing one red bandit." After a long pause the Air Boss replied, "Can you wait until all aircraft have landed?" I responded that would be fine.

As the last aircraft landed I accelerated to 500 knots for a low pass on the ship. We had closed to three miles when the Air Boss came up on the radio and told us the A-6 had broken a gear leg landing. We had to orbit and conserve our fuel until the Intruder was cleared out of the way. By then fuel was too low, and once again we were denied tradition.

The same warm response came from the men of *Connie* as canopies came up. Captain Ward said with a big grin, "You are making a habit of this, aren't you, Randy!" Five thousand handshakes later, Irish and I started on the mass of debriefings and paperwork. It almost wasn't worth shooting down the MiG for all the paperwork that followed!

Messages from all our buddies on other ships started pouring into the squadron. The Falcons' enlisted troops held a surprise party for us, complete with cake and ice cream. And when they painted the second MiG on my Pantom, they added a nice little V.C. truck!

Before wasting too much time, I fired off a message to Garry Weigand and Jim Rulefson: "And I'll get #3 before you get #2. Duke."

A thorn in the side cropped up before the night was over. The ABC and NBC television networks were aboard *Connie* shooting footage for release back home. That evening as Willie and I stood alert duty in our F-4, Lieutenant Gregg Southgate, one fine "scope," climbed up the ladder and said, "Duke, you have been relieved from alert. The press has set up an interview in strike operations."

I told Irish he could do what he wanted, but that my feelings we were still against interviews, due to the anti-war leftist slant. Expressing this to my skipper, Al Newman, I was told I had 100% backing to do what I desired. I did not attend the interview, going to Queenie's and Shoe's room instead for some papa charlie.

Shortly thereafter we heard a knock on the door. One of the civilian press representatives had come to ask if I would talk with him a few minutes off the record. After some serious consideration, I agreed. The first question was why I had refused on two different occasions to be interviewed. I frankly told him that most aircrews had been misquoted and that news services tended to be slightly left of center, giving more sympathy to Hanoi than to our men who were fighting and dying for what they believed. Very little attention was given to our views — it seemed McGovern, Fonda or Clark were always quoted at length.

The newsman set me back when he said, "Lieutenant Cunningham, that's what we would like to give you the chance to do." I told him that if I really thought my views would be expressed without bias, I would conduct an interview. But now that I was wound up, I took the opportunity to state some of my animosity toward the press. When Quang Tri City fell to North Vietnamese regulars, our newspapers and TV shows expounded on how the South Vietnamese troops often ran to leave the cities defenseless. Who wouldn't run when outnumbered two to one with no forthcoming relief or support? Yet there was a small three-inch column in the papers when the South Vietnamese paid a bloody price to retake Quang Tri.

The newsman apologized and agreed that much of what I said was true, but that NBC and ABC newsmen aboard had no such intentions. Nevertheless, the interview never took place.

Before the night was out we received the great news that our buddies in blue got two MiGs, a 19 and a 21, this day. The Gomers were finally coming out to play, and it was none too soon for Navy and Air Force fighter pilots.

The NVN pilot instructing his pupils has been reported as "Colonel Tomb." But he is probably Nguyen Van Bay, an early NVNAF ace credited with at least seven U.S. aircraft.

Chapter 7

Connie's A-7s were armed with a variety of ordnance on 9 May 1972, the day before our big battle with the MiGs. The center Corsair has bombs and an anti-radar Shrike missile plus a Sidewinder on the fuselage rail.

CHAPTER 7
MINING THE HARBORS

Throughout the war in Southeast Asia, foreign ships had crowded the harbors of the North delivering military supplies through Haiphong and other major ports of call. During October of 1971, we flew over Chinese and Russian ships loaded with surface-to-air missiles, fuel oil, tanks, MiG crates, and who knows what else. At times the ships would literally be clustered in tight.

There was little question among those of us who saw what was going on, as to the logical solution. But Nixon was vulnerable if he acted militarily. A Soviet response to any action he might take could jeopardize his plan for a Moscow summit in late May 1972, not to mention the reaction of the voluble anti-war segment in America.

Brian and I flew over these ships taking pictures of their lethal cargo, while the crews waved at us. They must have been laughing at our political stupidity in allowing them to deliver war materials that were killing our own people. Earlier in the war an Air Force pilot became so fed up with seeing his men killed because we could not prevent these cargo ships from delivering their deadly arms, that he fired at one. Although the pilot was quickly court martialed, many of us lauded his action, wishing he had blown the ship out of the water.

The rules of engagement for SEA were really something. We could bomb the supplies once they reached Laos or the South, but trucks are hard to find in the jungle. Inside the passes just over the North Vietnamese border, trucks were backed up for miles, waiting to run past our air attacks. Statements were often made about the North's ability to stop such a super power as the United States —with such strategic protection from our politicians, it was no wonder to us. North Vietnam would never have been able to launch a

This SAM was photographed by a photo-reconnaissance pilot — near miss! (USAF)

large-scale spring offensive if its supplies had been prevented from entering the harbors.

On May 8, 1972, the day of my second kill, President Nixon announced that major harbors in North Vietnam would be mined. Operation Linebacker missions into the North would be increased and more B-52 strikes would be laid on for military industrial targets.

The mines were deployed on May 9 with activation commencing in three days to give all foreign ships the opportunity to exit unharmed. A blanket warning was issued that any attempt to run the blockade would be dealt with severely. During the operation one of the most unusual kills of the war occurred when the cruiser *Chicago* launched a Talos missile at an attacking MiG to bring it down in flames.

The results of Nixon's action were graphic for us. Before the mining, strikes into the Haiphong area would bring numerous SAM launches (over 200) and heavy flak. After the mining, strikes into the same geography drew a maximum of four or five SAMs and less AAA.

The only disadvantage to the fighter crews was the MiGs' lack of fuel — we wanted them to get airborne so we could hassle. Somehow, though, that state of affairs was offset by the decline in enemy air defenses throughout the North and South. Eighty-five per cent of foreign supplies were prevented from reaching the enemy, or nearly 250,000 tons per month.

Again Brian and I were flying over Russian and Chinese ships —this time 20 to 30 of them were parked outside the harbors with their decks full, fearful of entering lest they fail to make it back out within the three-day deadline. They waved again, but this time we were the ones laughing.

The sophisticated AWT-I shipping mines were incredibly efficient. Some went off when metal neared; others would allow a ship to pass, giving the impression the area was clear, only to explode on a subsequent detection. Others were detonated by sound or pressure or who knows what secret gizmo. The North's spring offensive was halted due to this weapon and the air strikes launched against the existing supplies.

The Russians rattled their swords and directed a small fleet toward the Gulf of Tonkin, but Nixon called their bluff. As with most of us, he was sick of incidents such as those connected with the

Pueblo and a captured EC-121 crew in North Korea.

Some ingenious methods were attempted to get supplies in, such as unloading the cargo at sea onto sampans, but China and Russia made an end run by signing an agreement to open China's harbors. War materials were then transported overland to North Vietnam. Our bombers concentrated on bridges, road interdiction points, rail lines and other arteries of logistical supply.

In looking back over the pressures put upon our nation during the closing stages of the Vietnam War, I cannot help but believe that the majority of the American people were behind our final firm stand. As was obvious later, President Nixon had some basic defects in his character, but he understood the situation and acted accordingly. I wish he had acted sooner. If this was not what the nation wanted, I believe McGovern would have won the election.

Commander Eggert's F-4J, which Willie and I flew to bag our last three MiGs on 10 May. Each squadron in the air wing had a plane painted for the air group commander, and VF-96's number 100 was "borrowed" from the CAG.

Chapter 8

CHAPTER 8
TURKEY SHOOT

At 0830 on May 10, Lieutenant Curt Dose and his RIO, Lieutenant Commander Jim McDevitt, teamed up with Lieutenant Vaughn Hawkins and Lieutenant (jg) Charlie Tinker to form a TARCAP for a 35-plane Alpha Strike north of Haiphong. As the two F-4s escorted the force into the target, Red Crown called MiGs 35 miles northeast of Hanoi. Hawkins turned the section toward the threat, accelerated to 500 knots and set out for the hunt.

Bearing down on Kep airfield, they saw two MiG-21s rolling on the runway. Curt lined up the lead MiG just as it was liftig off and called, "Fox Two," as a Sidewinder went smoking away. The MiG driver was sharp. He turned into the missile, causing it to explode outside effective range.

Curt wasted no time. The 21 had bled off most of its energy from the break at low speed. Another 'Winder was squeezed off. The MiG attempted to out-turn the second missile, but it flew up the sleek fighter's tailpipe and blew up. The wreckage went fluttering down near the airfield.

Vaughn fired two Sidewinders at the trail MiG, but each one detonated aft of the enemy aircraft. A third Fox Two sent the MiG into a hard port turn, forcing "Hawk" to slide to the outside of the tight circle.

The pursuit was quickly ended when Curt called, "You have a 21 at six o'clock, Hawk!" Vaughn executed a vertical reversal, leaving both MiGs behind. The 21 which Hawk had been chasing fired an Atoll out of range.

Needless to say, all of us aboard ship were proud that another *Connie* squadron, VF-92, had entered the ranks of the MiG killers.

A little later that afternoon *Coral Sea's* VF-51 launched two

Phantoms to fly MiGCAP for a 30-plane strike group targeted on the Hai Duong railroad yards. Lieutenant Commander Chuck Schroder and RIO Lieutenant (jg) Dale Arends joined Lieutenants Ken Cannon and Rich Morris to form the MiG-hunting section. As the strike group went feet dry around Cam Pha, they pushed throttles forward and descended to 100 feet, behind a ridgeline for protection.

Then pandemonium broke loose over the radio — a tremendous MiG battle was taking place 30 miles north. The two Phantoms, ahead of the strike force, were heads up when they saw a parachute floating earthward from a burning MiG. Then a 21 appeared at three o'clock, Chuck turned toward it, and the Gomer ran.

The section reversed port toward the target just in time to see a MiG-17 sneaking in at ten o'clock. Chuck maneuvered to the bandit's six o'clock as the MiG went into a hard port turn. Ken zoomed high over the engaged fighter to clear his wingman's rear. As Chuck started to squeeze the trigger, the 17 executed a high-G, nose-low turn, forcing the F-4 out in front. Chuck calmly called, "Okay, he's at my six now," as he lit the burners and pulled out of the MiG's missile range.

The Gomer made a hard turn away, looking for the other F-4, but it was too late. Ken sent off a Sidewinder to destroy the MiG.

The morning of May 10th began as any other for me. As I made my way up to the catwalk surrounding the flight deck, I noticed the ever-present low, wispy clouds that hugged the humid Gulf — always a beautiful sight with the sun coming up. Early morning at sea has held man fascinated for centuries. There's nothing like the smell of salt spray — of course one had to get upwind of the ship to get an unadulterated whiff. All Navy ships have that curious combination of smells: salt water and fuel oil.

With the beginning of Operation Linebacker, and now the mining, apprehension dominated my thoughts. I suppose all fighter pilots like to think of themselves as indestructable, unbeatable, fearless. . . but my mind would wander back to home, my wife and child and the possibility that I might never see them again. I fought back tears and a lump in my throat often. This brooding had come over me the morning of the 10th, only more consuming. A few days earlier I had received a "Dear John" letter from my wife. She wanted out of the marriage. The strain was almost unbearable. Just when I was feeling sorriest for myself, a voice bounced in. . . "Hey,

Duke! What you doin', eatin' more bullets?"

Irish! We were close enough to count on each other in times of trouble, though we had our arguments, both in and out of the cockpit. The moment of brooding introspection was gone. As time went on our friendship grew stronger and later I was to find Willie a major support in keeping me up, when personal problems became almost unbearable. The Irishman was always there.

The ship was waking up. Cat crews tested the catapults in the roaring, hissing steam. Ordnance crews strained to load the 500-and 1,000-pound bombs as sweat glistened on their backs. Fuel was pumped into the aircraft. Other pilots had come topside to watch, perhaps to think a little too much about where they were going, as I was.

As Irish and I walked down the flight deck, the enlisted crews looked up with "Hi, Mr. Cunningham; Hi, Mr. Driscoll... What's the target? Will ya give 'em one for our POWs? And watch out for yourself." What a fantastic feeling — I honestly think, in retrospect, I valued most the friendship of these men who made possible what we did in the air.

Going down the ladder into the flight crew mess, we found Ramerez waiting to cook one of his gourmet omelets. Lieutenant Carl Snodgrass, the squadron's reason for success, wasn't letting breakfast get in the way of his clucking and checking over the status of our F-4s. He was an inspiration to all of us, even though he didn't fly: a true professional responsible for our aircraft's being in such top condition.

After Willie put down enough to feed the Irish Army, we headed for strike operations. Entering the room, we found a curious lack of the usual hustle and bustle, the jokes and laughter. Everyone's eyes were riveted to the strike board with a line running into enemy territory. The target was the Haiphong railyard that served as a funneling point for the Ban Kori, Mugia and Napi mountain passes leading to the Ho Chi Minh Trail. It was smack in the middle of several MiG fields — Phuc Yen, Kep and Yen Bai on the way in; Dong Suong, Bai Thuong, Thanh Hoa and Vinh on the way out. And the target itself was supposed to be heavily fortified with AAA ranging from 23mm to 120mm, not to mention SAMs along the flight path.

Regardless, the F-4 crews were bantering about who would get

Here we're strapping into "Showtime 100" for the mission to Hai Duong rail yard, little knowing that we'd return as aces; minus Gus Eggert's airplane!

the MiGCAP because the enemy was sure to be up in force. Since the skipper had had his turn at the coveted position, the XO and his "wingie" took the CAP with Matt Connelly and Dave Erickson forming the other section. Steve Shoemaker was to escort the A-7 SAM suppression aircraft. Then it dawned on me that Willie and I hadn't made the schedule! Shoe glanced over, "Hey, Duke, what's the matter? Ya can't make 'em all, you know."

The skipper looked over and smiled as he added our names to the strike roster as flak suppressers. Even though we'd be loaded with Rockeye bombs and would stay with the slower attack birds, once the bombs were away, we still had four Sidewinder and two Sparrow stingers if the MiGs should want to play. It seemed so important for us to go, but then there were mixed feelings when our names were added, "Maybe it's not such a good idea, at that." That old mixture of apprehension and aggressiveness.

We had the remainder of the morning for strike planning, target analysis and aircrew briefings. SAM sites had to be plotted along with flight route. Tanking, rendezvous, ingress and egress had to be prepared. Pictures of each target had to be memorized and studied to eliminate the possibility of bombing non-military areas. Flight gear and survival equipment had to be checked. As busy as all this kept us, we still had to wait a few hours before the mission with nothing to keep our minds occupied. No question that this was the worst time of the day as anxiety crept in to keep us company.

I tried to hide its reality by telling myself that I was simply tired; that the funny feeling in my stomach was from Ramerez's spicy food. Walking up on the flight deck I saw one guy so entrenched in anxiety he lost his breakfast over the side. A quote from George Bernard Shaw seemed to fit into the situation, "If a man cannot look evil in the face without illusion, he will never know what it really is or combat it effectually."

Still, I don't guess any of us would have gone if he had not felt that it was the other guy who would get hit. And I can honestly say, though we may have been outnumbered, our intense air combat training had instilled confidence in us. My Navy training is the reason I'm alive today, and I thank the Navy officials who had enough foresight to offer us an energetic tactical flight program.

The time arrived to man our aircraft. The edge of my anxiety was, for the most part, gone as I preflighted my Phantom, trying to

The MiG-17 allegedly flown by "Colonel Tomb." We shot down three 17s on our final mission, and perhaps this green-camouflaged bird was one of them.

appear composed. Blast it all! I tripped over the tie-down chain again! Irish roared with laughter, showing no sympathy whatsoever to my downed ego. This fighter jock nonchalance I was prone to displaying had no place here — all it did was embarrass me.

All strapped in, we waited for the start-engines call in the 100% humidity. Word filtered down the line there might be a cancellation due to bad weather, making me fume, but the order soon came that the mission was a go.

Turbines whined as they picked up speed and aircraft were rolling up to the cat. Jet blast deflectors went up and the first aircraft was off. One by one, each took his turn on one of the four catapults until it was our turn. Hooked onto the cat, we ran up to 100% power, checked the instruments, lit the burners, saluted the cat officer and, wham... we were on our way, doing nearly 200 knots in just a few hundred feet.

We quickly accelerated to 400 knots for the climb to the tanker. Topping off, the group got into formation as Commander Eggert set course for the target. After being feet wet over the Gulf of Tonkin for about 15 minutes we approached the North Vietnamese coast near the Red River — the enemy was busily scanning us with radar.

Brian and I were stepped up above the main strike force of A-6s and A-7s. Irish commented on what a shame such a beautiful country had to be bombed — winding waterways glistened through emerald green valleys as the sun reflected off the roofs of the populated wetlands.

As we approached the target, the attack aircraft went sailing over it. CAG called and told them they had gone too far, so they rolled back in from west to east, looking for all the world like a column of ants as they went down the chute. As the rest of us orbited overhead, AAA puffs dotted the sky. Commander Harry Blackburn, who was right across the circle from me, took a hit by 85mm. His RIO, Steve Rudluff, survived to spend the remainder of the war as a POW. His wingman was hit by the same barrage, and he went out single-engine. MiG-21s made one pass at him, then let him go.

The first attack aircraft had demolished the primary target, so CAG directed the remainder of the strike force to secondary targets. Brian and I were sent to the large supply area adjacent to the railyard. We decided to close in tight to fighting wing formation and release simultaneously. We rolled over just as two SAMs were

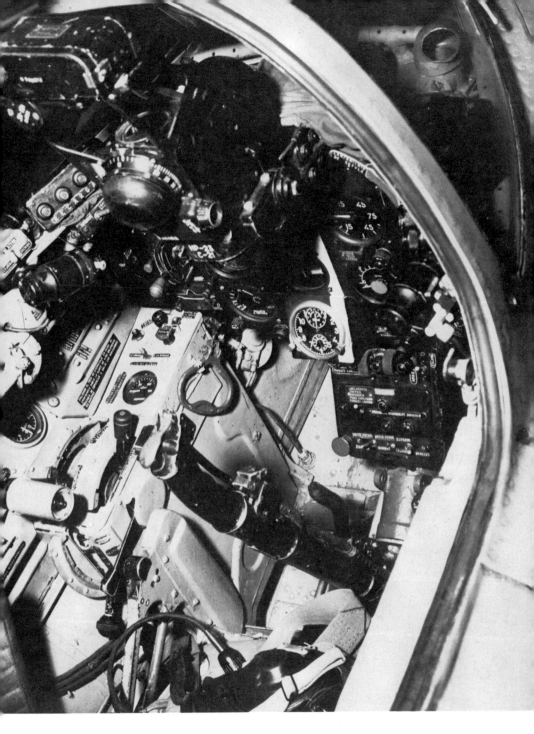

A defecting Cuban pilot flew a MiG-17 to Homestead AFB, Florida in 1969. Here's a cockpit shot, identical (except Spanish placards) to 17s flown by the NVAF. (USAF)

launched at us; failing to track, they came whizzing up past us. I looked back down at the target in time to see it disappear in a cloud of smoke and debris — A-7 1,000-pounders had leveled it flat.

We rolled over a bit more and I picked up a long red brick storage building. Dropping our bombs, we pulled off the target and I made the mistake of looking back over my right shoulder to see what we had done to the target. My head was down and locked when Brian, being the superb wingman he was, called, "Duke, you have MiG-17s at your seven o'clock, shooting!"

Two 17s flew right by Brian's F-4, about 500 feet away, and I was about 1,000 feet in front! I popped my wing back down and reversed hard port in time to see a 17 pull in behind and start firing. That damn 37mm put out a BB the size of a pumpkin (in two days the thing surely had grown from the grapefruit size of the May 8th mission), and a muzzle flash that seemed to jet out the length of a football field!

My first instinct was to break into him. Then I thought, "I did that two days ago and the guy rendezvoused on me." A quick glance at the MiG told me it was closing on me at high speed, meaning controls that were hard to move. I broke into him, anyway.

The MiG driver just didn't have the muscle to move that stick. He overshot over the top to my two o'clock, but his wingman, who was back about 1,500 feet, pitched up and did a vertical displacement roll out to my belly side. "Duke," Brian called, "I'll take care of the guy at your six." With utter confidence in Brian, I turned my attention back to the other MiG. When I squeezed off a Sidewinder the enemy fighter was well within minimum range, but by the time the missile got to him he was about 2,500 feet out in front of me. . . that's how fast he was going. The 'Winder blew him to pieces. That engagement had lasted about 15 seconds.

On two previous occasions Brian had dragged MiGs out for me on his tail. . . now it was my turn to reciprocate: "Brian, here's your chance. I'm gonna drag this guy for you." I started accelerating down in a turn with the MiG hot after me. "Brian, get that S.O.B....Brian?"

"I can't help you, Duke, I've got two on my tail." With a quick disengagement maneuver I lost my pursuer, accelerating out to 600 knots. Looking off to my right, there was Brian! He had seen me take off, shook off his two MiGs in the same fashion, and pulled back into combat spread position. There simply could not have been a better wingman on all the earth.

We had all kinds of fuel left (the centerline tanks had just finished transferring), so we pitched up into the vertical, came over the top at 15,000 feet and rolled out of the Immelmann back into the fight. I saw Matt Connelly and his RIO, Tom Blonski, chasing a 17 which soon burst into flames — the pilot ejected before the stricken fighter smashed into the ground.

We were going pretty fast, worrying about jettisoning the centerlines — we had had some problems with them hitting the stabilator in high speed jettisons. But thinking again, we blew the tanks anyway.

The scene below was straight out of *The Dawn Patrol*. There were eight MiG-17s in a defensive wheel with three F-4s mixed in! Our guys should never have been in there . . . they were down to 350 knots, a good place to die. I called for Brian to cover and rolled in.

I no more got my nose pointed down when a Phantom came out of the circle, missing us by a hair! "Willie, who's in 112?" It was Dwight Timm, the XO, with Jim Fox in his backseat. "Jeez, look at that!" I blurted out. Timm was in a port turn with a MiG-17 about 2,000 feet behind him, a MiG-21 about 1,000 feet behind the 17, and what he didn't see, a 17 on his belly side, flying wing!

We were back at seven o'clock, behind the trailing MiGs, but the real threat was the 17 flying wing, about to pull in and start shooting. I called for him to maneuver his fighter and got a tone to shoot, but the XO was in burner — if I squeezed off a Fox Two it would most likely go for the Phantom.

I called for him to reverse starboard to kick the MiG across his tail, underneath, allowing my Sidewinder to home on the MiG's tailpape. He thought I was talking about the trailing MiGs (he still hadn't spotted the real threat), so he kept on going. I called again, "Showtime, reverse starboard! If you don't, you're going to die!"

"Duke," strained Willie, "we have four MiG-17s at our seven o'clock." They were out of range, but Timm's arcing turn was allowing them slowly to gain on us! Willie was on the ball, "Duke, look at two o'clock high!" I looked up and saw two flashes. . . not airplanes, just flashes, since they were too high. "There can't be anymore 17s in the world!" my mind retorted. I was right, they weren't 17s; they were MiG-19s!

As they rolled in on us, guns firing, I reversed, and they went out to our six o'clock. This put the fight over to our ten o'clock with a deep lag position to the MiG behind Timm, but out of range of the MiGs which had been trailing us. . . except for one just about in the firing position.

One of the only things I did right that day was to have about 550 knots just then. The MiG behind me couldn't close as long as I didn't turn too tight — at 500 knots I was opening on him. The problem was, I had to turn to stay behind Timm and his MiG. I told Willie to keep an eye on that MiG and tell me when it started to pull lead. As it did so, shooting those blasted BBs, I'd straighten out and open the gap a bit. This all happened in the space of a few seconds.

I was still screaming for Timm to break starboard when Irish called out, "Duke, look up at nine o'clock!" There, 4,000 feet above us, I saw four MiG-21s just cruising along, content to keep an eye on the fight below — probably didn't want to get in the way of all those BBs!

Finally, Timm broke. I had a tone. . . no tone. . . then a tone again. I squeezed the trigger, "Fox Two!" Jim Fox looked out of his back seat in Timm's Phantom and for the first time he saw the MiG. . .just as the missile hit. He said the lethal heat seeker traveled the entire length of the 17, blowing it to bits. Commander Timm's wife later rewarded me with a super-sized kiss.

The pilot ejected behind the F-4, and I had to break hard port and drop the wing to miss him. As soon as the missile hit the MiG-17, the four 21s above rolled in on us. They must have been pretty upset when I popped their comrade, who would probably end up driving water buffalo down the Ho Chi Minh trail. As they rolled in, I pulled hard into them, putting them 180° off me. Timm was already on the deck and heading for the coast, not a bad place to go — everywhere I looked there were MiGs and no F-4s, so I headed east myself.

At the same time Matt Connelly was downing his second MiG of the day. An A-7 driver who had pulled off target and headed toward the coast heard the MiG call. He decided he wanted to see a MiG just once, so he turned around. He came through the fight with two MiG-17s on his tail. Matt shot one off and told the Corsair pilot to get the hell out, that the A-7 was no match for MiGs. The A-7 headed out, but a few minutes later back it came with two more MiGs in trail! Matt knocked another MiG off the A-7 pilot's tail, who got the hint and hauled his aircraft out towards the Gulf.

The Shoeman and his RIO, Keith Crenshaw, spotted a MiG-17

This MiG-17 was shot down near Hanoi in October 1967 — looks good from this view!. (USAF) going after an F-4. With high angle-off, he fired a Sidewinder that missed, but forced the MiG off the Phantom's tail. Matt pitched up into the vertical with another MiG as Tom, his RIO, called, "Matt, look at nine o'clock: MiG-17" They were so close Matt said he could identify the Gomer if they ever met. Both fighters slowed down to less than 175 knots and the MiG disengaged. Wisely, Matt elected not to pursue the nimble adversary from his low energy state.

As Matt headed out for the coast, Shoe and Keith were busy losing a MiG that had perched on their Phantom's tail. Steve lost the MiG, but in the process he also lost all his instruments and navigational aids, ending up at 50 feet doing 550 knots. Not much help to visual reference. Thinking he was heading for the coast, he found himself on the outskirts of Hanoi.

A prompt reversal and Steve was heading back with strong SAM radar indications on the ECM gear. Peering out at 12 o'clock he saw an SA-2 heading straight for him. Playing a game of aerial chicken, he broke hard at the last moment, forcing the SAM to miss. Before the day was over, he blasted a MiG-17 out of the air.

As Willie and I smoked past I told him, "It sure is a shame to quit when we have all this gas and there are all kinds of MiGs." So far the whole fight had taken only about two minutes. Then I thought of how badly we were outnumbered. . . and we had become separated from Brian. Yeah, it was a good time to get out.

As we headed for the coast at 10,000 feet, I spotted another airplane on the nose, slightly low, heading straight for us. It was a MiG-17. I told Irish to watch how close we could pass the MiG to take out as much lateral separation as possible so he could not convert as easily to our six o'clock. We used to do the same thing against the A-4s back at Miramar since the two aircraft were virtually identical in performance. This proved to be my first near-fatal mistake. . . A-4s don't have guns in the nose.

The MiG's entire nose lit up like a Christmas tree! Pumpkin-sized BBs went sailing by our F-4. I pulled sharply into the pure vertical to destroy the Gomer's tracking solution. As I came out of the six-G pullup I strained to see the MiG below as my F-4 went straight up. I was sure it would go into a horizontal turn, or just run as most had done in the past.

As I looked back over my ejection seat I got the surprise of my life: there was the MiG, canopy to canopy with me, barely 300 feet away!

In all, VF-96 shot down six MiGs in the fight of 10 May. Back in the squadron ready room, Tom Blonski (left) and Matt Connelly describe how they bagged two 17s. On the right is John "Baby Lizard" Anderson, a good friend and good pilot.

I could see a Gomer leather helmet, Gomer goggles, Gomer scarf...
and his intent Gomer expression. I began to feel numb. My stomach
grabbed at me in knots. There was no fear in this guy's eyes as we
zoomed some 8,000 feet straight up.

I lit the afterburners and started to outclimb my adversary, but
this excess performance placed me above him. As I started to pull
over the top, he began shooting. My second near-fatal mistake — I
had given him a predictable flight path, and he had taken advantage
of it. I was forced to roll and pull to the other side. He pulled in right
behind me.

Not wanting to admit this guy was beating me, I blurted to Willie,
"That S.O.B. is really lucky! All right, we'll get this guy now!" I
pulled down to accelerate with the MiG at my four o'clock. I watched
and waited until he committed his nose down, then pulled up into
him and rolled over the top, placing me at his five o'clock. Even
though I was too close with too much angle-off his tail to fire a
missile, the maneuver placed me in an advantageous position. I
thought I had outflown him —overconfidence replaced fear.

I pulled down, holding top rudder, to press for a shot, and he
pulled up into me, shooting! I thought, "Oh, no maybe this guy isn't
just lucky after all!" He used the same maneuver I had attempted,
pulling up into me and forcing an overshoot — we were in the classic
rolling scissors. As his nose committed I pulled up into him.

In training I had fought in the same situation. I learned if my
opponent had his nose too high, I could snap down, using the one G to
advantage, then run out to his six o'clock before he could get turned
around and get in range.

As we slowed to 200 knots I knew it was time to bug out.
Lieutenant Dave Frost, a Top Gun instructor, had taught me how to
disengage in this situation. He was one of the smartest fighter pilots
I've ever known. The MiG's superior turn radius, coupled with
higher available G at that speed, started giving him a constant
advantage. When he raised his nose just a bit too high, I pulled into
him. Placing my aircraft nearly 180° to follow, Willie and I were two
miles ahead of him, out of his missile range, at 600 knots airspeed.

With our energy back, I made a 60° nose-up vertical turn back into
the pressing MiG. He climbed right after us, and, again, with the
Phantom's superior climbing ability, I outzoomed him as he
squirted BBs in our direction. it was a carbon copy of the first

engagement seconds earlier as we went into another rolling scissors.

Again we were forced to disengage as advantage and disadvantage traded sides. As we blasted away to regain energy for the second time, Irish came up on the itercom, "Hey, Duke, how ya doin' up there? This guy really knows what he's doin'. Maybe we ought to call it a day."

This almost put me into a blind rage. To think some Gomer had not only stood off my attacks but had gained an advantage on me twice!

"Hang on, Willie. We're gonna get this guy!"

"Go get him, Duke. I'm right behind you!"

Irish was all over the cockpit, straining to keep sight of the MiG as I pitched back toward him for the third time. Man, it felt good to have that second pair of eyes back there, especially with an adversary who knew what air fighting was all about. Very seldom did U.S. fighter pilots find a MiG that fought in the vertical. The enemy liked to fight in the horizontal for the most part, or just to run, if he didn't have the advantage.

Once again I met the MiG-17 head-on, this time with an offset so he couldn't use his guns. As I pulled up into the pure vertical I could again see this determined pilot a few feet away. Winston Churchill once wrote, "In war, if you are not able to beat your enemy at his own game, it is nearly always better to adopt some striking variant." My mind simply came up with a last-ditch idea. I pulled hard toward his aircraft and yanked the throttles back to idle, popping the speed brakes at the same time.

The MiG shot out in front of me for the first time! The Phantom's nose was 60° above the horizon with airspeed down to 150 knots in no time. I had to go to full burner to hold my position. The surprised enemy pilot attempted to roll up on his back above me. Using only rudder to avoid stalling the F-4 with the spoilers on the wings, I rolled to the MiG's blind side. He attempted to reverse his roll, but as his wings banked sharply he must have stalled the aircraft momentarily and his nose fell through, placing me at his six but still too close for a shot. "This is no place to be with a MiG-17," I thought, "at 150 knots. . . this slow, he can take it right away from you."

But he had stayed too long. We later found out that this superb fighter pilot, later identified as "Colonel Tomb" of the North Vietnamese Air Force, had refused to disengage when his GCI controller ordered him to return to base. After the war we found out that "Tomb", presumably with 13 American aircraft to his credit, had to run for it if he were going to get down before flaming out.

He pitched over the top and started straight down. I pulled hard over and followed. Though I didn't think a Sidewinder would guide straight down, with the heat of the ground to look at, I called "Fox Two" and squeezed one off. The missile came off the rail and went straight to the MiG. There was just a little flash and I thought it had missed him. As I started to fire my last Sidewinder, there was an abrupt burst of flame. Black smoke erupted from the 17. He didn't seem to go out of control. . . the fighter simply kept descending, crashing into the ground at about a 45° angle.

"Duke, check ten o'clock; MiG-17 rolling in on us!" Irish had his eyes open. We had 550 knots, so I pulled nose high into the attacking craft and told Willie, "Here comes number six." Just then Matt, who had been watching the fight, yelled out, "Duke, get the hell out of there! There are four 17s at your seven o'clock!"

I saw Matt with his nose on us, just as he fired a missile. I thought, "Matt, Jeez, you're shooting at us!" His Sparrow went right over our tail and back to our seven o'clock. . . where four 17s were in pursuit! Matt's desperate missile shot did the trick as the Sparrow went sailing into the center of the formation — they looked like fleas evacuating a dog, splitting off in every direction to get out of the way.

"That's it, baby," I said. "We got five. . . that's all I want. We're getting out of here!" We rolled and headed for the coast with Matt on our wing. To our left a heavy barrage of 85mm blackened the sky. ECM gear said SAMs were on the way, also. Two of them raced for us head-on, but we were able to defeat them as they roared past our nose.

Then a sudden lull. Something was wrong when enemy gunners just plain quit firing. Willie found the reason, "Duke! MiGs chasing us!" As I pitched up there was a 21 smack in front of the windscreen. I was going to shoot, but he was well within minimum range, so I couldn't. I flew right by him. . . I had a windscreen full of MiG-21. Before I could comprehend what was happening, a MiG-17 flashed by within close range and then yet another 17. If I'd had a gun I might have made three more kills.

I pitched off, broke and headed out again in burner. As we neared Nam Dinh I heard another SAM call. Glancing over to starboard I watched an SA-2 heading straight for us. Before I could maneuver the SAM went off. The resultant concussion was not too violent but

Willie and I have just stepped off the Marine helo upon return to *Connie* after narrowly avoiding capture off the NVN coast. It was good to be greeted by Gus Eggert, the CAG, and our squadron CO, Al Newman.

my head felt like it went down to my stomach. We had had closer SAM explosions than that and there appeared to be no damage. I immediately went to the gauges to check for systems malfunctions. Everything indicated normal so I continued to climb, watching for more SAMs. Irish couldn't understand how the thing got so close without our ECM gear's warning us. Neither could I.

About 45 seconds later the aircraft yawed violently to the left. "What's the matter, Duke? You flying instruments again?" asked Irish. I steadied up and looked into the cockpit to see the PC-1 hydraulic system indicating zero, the PC-2 and utility systems fluctuating. Fear, that ever present companion, wanted to run the ship, "What now, Cunningham?" raced through my mind.

Thank God for sea stories, for somewhere out of my memory bank came the recollection that "Duke" Hernandez, another Navy pilot, had rolled his aircraft to safety after losing his hydraulics. When an F-4 loses hydraulics the stabilator locks, forcing the aircraft's nose to pitch straight up: the stick has no effect on the controls, only rudder and power are available when this happens.

Sure enough, when PC-2 went to zero, the nose went straight up! I pushed full right rudder, yawing the nose to the right and forcing the nose down. As the nose passed through the horizon I selected idle on the throttle and put out the speed brakes to prevent a power dive.

I quickly transferred to left rudder, yawing the nose through the downswing to force it above the horizon. Full afterburner, retract speed brakes and the F-4 was in a climbing half roll. Just before the F-4 stalled at the top, the process was repeated.

I rolled the Phantom 20 miles in this manner — I have no idea how many times, since all I cared about was making it to the water —beginning at 27,000 and working down to 17,000 by the time we reached the Red River Valley with wall-to-wall villages. The most fear I've ever known in my life was thinking that Irish and I were going to become POWs, especially if the Gomers knew we had become the first American aces of the Vietnam War.

The aircraft was burning just aft of Irish — I told him to reselect the ejection sequence handle so that if he decided to go, I wouldn't go with him. He asked why. I told him I wasn't about to spend nine or ten years in the Hanoi Hilton. "Okay, Duke," replied Irish, "I'm staying with you until you give the word, but I'm placing the ejection handle so that we both go when I eject."

The next few seconds were full of fear — I even prayed, asking God to get me out of this. The aircraft rolled out, and I thought He didn't have anything to do with it. Then the F-4 rolled uncontrollably again, and I thought to myself, "God, I didn't mean it!"

An explosion ripped through the Phantom and I almost ejected, but we were still over land. The radio was full of screams from our buddies to punch out. They knew the burning F-4 could explode any second. A-7s and F-4s were all around us — I caught glimpses of them as we rolled up and down. Any MiG wandering within 10 miles of the area would have been sorry; a situation like this gets pilots hopping mad.

Just as we crossed the coast we lost our last utility system and another violent explosion shook our fighter. A few seconds earlier and we would have been forced to come down in enemy territory. Someone up there must have heard my prayer. At that moment I prayed the classic "foxhole prayer" and pledged to myself that I would seek to understand and accept Jesus Christ if I made it.

With the hydraulics gone, the rudder was useless. On the upswing I was unable to force the nose back down. The F-4 stalled and went into a spin.

Each revolution I could see land, then ocean; incredible as it may seem, my fear kept me in the aircraft. I thought we were too close to the beach and the winds normally blew landward. I told Irish to stay with me for two more turns as I attempted to break the spin and get some more water behind us. I deployed the drag chute with no effect — the controls were limp.

Willie and I had often discussed what we would do should the need ever arise to leave our aircraft. I would say, "Irish, eject, eject, eject" and he would pull the cord on the third "eject."

"We are going to have to get out" finally left my mouth.

"Duke, the handle is set. . . when I go, you're going with me. Good luck."

I got out, "Irish, e-. . ." and I heard his seat fire. There is only a split second delay between the rear and front seats firing — if the front went out first the rocket motor would fry the guy in back — but I heard his canopy go and thought my seat had malfunctioned. As I started to reach for the ejection cord, my seat fired, driving me up the rail and away from Showtime 100.

There was no pain from the G loading, then everything became quiet as I tumbled through space. I caught a glimpse of Willie's chute opening and, again, felt fear over the fact that something was not going to work and that I would not separate from my seat. But everything worked as advertised and I sailed away from the bulky seat.

The chute lines rushed past me — I must have been going down head first — then the chute opened with a crack-the-whip jolt. Sharp pain ran through my back.

Beautiful, a full canopy, but the first thing I looked for was land —was I drifting toward it? The choking fear of capture grabbed me again as I saw enemy patrol boats, a large freighter and some junks coming out of the Red River toward us. I just knew I had no taste for pumpkin soup.

Totally fixated on the boats, I was startled by the intrusion of Corsairs and Phantoms rolling in on the enemy vessels. Hey, they hadn't left us — and I knew they were low on fuel, yet they pressed through AAA and SAMs to turn the boats around. I felt small and alone floating down in my chute until my buddies made their presence known. I find it hard even now to express the gratitude that flooded my senses.

Then it dawned on me that I had a survival radio! I could talk! "May Day, May Day! This is Showtime. 100 Alpha is okay." (Willie was 100 Bravo.)

"Hang on, sailor, we're on our way," replied the SAR team. Wow! In my joy I looked around for the first time. The biggest boost of the day was to see Irish a few hundred feet away waving like crazy to let me know he was okay. he flipped me the bird... no doubt about it, he was fine. I cordially returned the "salute."

We were really coming down slow, plenty of time to go through all the procedures we'd been taught, but never had to use until now. Then, for some unknown reason, my thoughts shifted to home and the "Dear John" letter from my wife. I seriously questioned if I would have what it takes to go through the camps if I were captured. We had been told the two major sustaining forces in captivity would be a strong faith in God and a loving wife. I was deficient in both areas.

Thinking about my wife, I cried like a baby for a minute or so. My life was falling apart in great emotional upheaval. Again, I vowed to change my life for the better if I got out of this.

My mind jolted back to the present difficulties when the wind caught my survival raft hanging several feet below me on a tether. I started to swing back and forth lake a pendulum. At the top of each swing the side of my chute would tuck under and, having never parachuted before, I thought it would fold up and let me fall. The para-riggers later told me it was perfectly safe, but it served admirably in taking my mind off personal problems.

About 20 feet above the water I jettisoned the parachute while looking down at my raft. I went belly first into the warm, muddy water. Muddy? Struggling to the surface I found myself right in the mouth of the Red River! In scrambling for the tether attached to the raft I noticed something floating in the water next to me. A closer look revealed a rotting Vietnamese corpse, apparently washed down the river. For a second I thought it was Willie, but the body was too good looking. I swam for my raft with Olympic speed.

Irish was later asked by the Boston press, "When you were hanging in your parachute after killing three North Vietnamese pilots and bombing their country, and after being shot down and nearly killed, what was going through your mind?" Sensing the left leanings of the interviewer, Willie replied, "My thoughts were that perhaps I had made an incorrect decision in leaving the Army Reserve in Boston." Needless to say, the laughter overwhelmed the interviewer, who retired discretely.

We were in the water 15 minutes pending 15 years, when three Marine helos from USS *Okinawa* hovered over. As fighter pilots, we used to make jokes about those funny little machines with rotors that chugged along just over 100 knots. My views changed radically at that moment.

We were aboard in no time and on our way to the hospital ship. The President couldn't have been treated better. Everyone from the ship's cook to the CO came by to say hello and to ask if we needed anything. Doctors swarmed over us and we were checked for injuries. My back was stiff and out of place, but pronounced okay, so we boarded the helo again to get back to *Connie*.

As we circled CVA-64, we could see the decks lined with waving, cheering men. As we gently set down the cheers were audible above the chopper's roar. My back was throbbing, but damned if I were going to be carried aboard on a stretcher. Irish helped me out of the chopper. By the time I had my feet in *Connie's* deck the tears were flowing — Irish, too. It was impossible to express our joy at being home and not under a V.C. gun.

I think all 5,000 guys on the ship were waiting for us. Captain Ward, Al Newman and Dwight Timm ran over to help us off that sweet Marine helo. A few of the men looking on made no effort to hide their tears. A black enlisted trooper made his way over and said, "Mr. Cunningham, it's nice that you shot down three MiGs today, and it's nice you became the first ace, but from the men of *Connie*, we're just glad to have you back, sir." As emotionally charged as all of us were, it would not have taken much to break me down, but this gesture was overwhelming.

The next few hours were full of debriefs, paper work and congratulations. Later at the evening meal some of the attack pilots walked over. "Hey, Duke, remember when we said that all you F-4 drivers were good for was taking our gas or flying our wing? Well, we take it back." It was more than nice to have these attack guys around risking their lives to keep the enemy away when Irish and I were in so much trouble. Their spirit, dedication and professional ability couldn't be matched as far as I was concerned.

The night of May 10th I fought a restless battle in my mind. The events of a few hours previous seemed like a dream, though my physical exhaustion proved their reality. As I lay in the dark hospital room, isolated and feeling very alone, my wife's letter saying it was over between us crept again into my thoughts, with memories of my handsome young son, Randall Todd. I was punched full of empty holes in considering what was to become of my life.

I don't know what "Quack" (an affectionate name given to Dr. Rienheld) gave me, but thankfully, it worked. The next thing I remember was being awakened by our duty officer — "Duke, you have 30 minutes to get yourself ready to catch a plane for Saigon and news interviews."

"Look, go tell the CO that my ideas haven't changed about talking with the press. I'm not going!"

It didn't take long for my squadronmate to return, "Duke, the CO would like to talk to you." Admiral Cooper explained that we had waited a long time to beat the Air Force in producing an ace, and that he highly recommended that I attend the news briefing. He said I could do the services some good in our divided nation, so I accepted.

As we walked up to the flight deck, the men were assembled, waiting to wish us well. One trooper gave me a shirt to wear, reading, "Gen. Robin Olds 4, Duke 5," indicating my trump of the

Though my back was hurting from the ejection, I took a few minutes to relax with Willie following our return to *Constellation*.

man who had been the leading MiG killer in Southeast Asia since 1967.

That was the last time I had the opportunity to serve with this great gathering of men. I still write some of them. Bonds so strong are difficult to break.

May 10, 1972 had been quite a day for both the Navy and the Air Force. "Turkey Shoot" was certainly the proper term — eight MiGs fell to Navy pilots, six of those kills belonging to my squadron, VF-96. The 555th Tactical Fighter Squadron, the famous "Triple Nickel" of the USAF, downed three MiGs and one of those was the first kill made by the team of Captains Steve Ritchie and Chuck DeBellevue. Steve went on to get five kills as a pilot, while Chuck ended the war with six as a Weapons Systems Officer, the equivalent of the Navy RIO.

Chapter 9

A repainted F-4J became the new "Showtime 100," with VF-96's eight MiG kills noted on the intake.

CHAPTER 9
HOME

As our small C-2 transport flew southward over the Gulf of Tonkin, Irish was taking in the view of lush jungle to the east. It was almost placid except for smoke rising over the war-torn countryside. As the mail plane touched down on the sweltering runway at Saigon and taxied toward the air terminal, I still had misgivings about a press conference.

The Navy PR people who greeted us said news correspondents from all over the world would be present to talk with the first American aces in almost 20 years. I had assumed that various restrictions would be placed upon our commentary, but I was wrong. We were told to express our thoughts openly unless the subject matter involved classified information. A military advisor would stand by, but only if Willie or I asked for help was he to step in.

Once seated before the reporters my apprehension and nervousness changed to curiosity at my first chance to monitor the interests of the foreign news media. Except for one American and one French correspondent, the atmosphere was friendly. These two guys were after bear, asking leading questions such as "Do you think this is a worthwhile war?" "Who would you support in a presidential election?" "Do you get satisfaction out of shooting down airplanes?" I felt these questions unworthy of an answer, but other questions came out of the group that I felt free to address.

"Were the enemy pilots any good?"

"The North Vietnamese pilots were poorly trained. They went to Russia or China for pilot training and I feel the Russian tactical doctrines are poor. The pilots got little air combat tactics training and little if any training against dissimilar types of aircraft. Overall, their pilots were inferior to our Air Force and Navy pilots, but each air arm has its Red Barons. The last guy I met was one of the best, having gained the advantaqge on me twice before I could get away and shoot him down."

"Were Russian pilots flying the MiGs?"

"To my knowledge, Russian pilots served as advisors only. They did not engage in combat during the latter stages of the war, but we did face North Korean pilots."

"What do you think of the MiG as a fighter?"

"The MiG is a beautiful lady; a bit crude, but still a lady. Any airplane is like a man's wife — she has her good points and her bad points. We learn to live with the bad points and love the good ones. The MiG-17 is the most difficult to shoot down because of its unbelievable turn rate. The North Vietnamese used it as their dogfight plane while the MiG-21 was used primarily as an interceptor. If the Phantom or Crusader plays the 17's game of a slow turning fight, then the 17 will no doubt win with equal pilots and fuel considerations. One good MiG-17 driver can hold off two Phantoms if he can keep them in sight. On the other hand, any of our fighters can get away from the 17 unless critically low and slow. The pilot's ability is, however, the most important criterion. The MiG-21 is a better weapons platform than the F-4 at speeds below 450 knots or above 20,000 feet. The 21's weak points lie in lack of fuel and poor weapons systems. His Atoll is similar to our older model heat-seeking Sidewinder and his gunsight is antiquated. In combat it has been seen that the Vietnamese and Arab pilots are the reason for its poor success, not the plane itself. If I had my choice of aircraft in a dogfight, I'd have to go with the MiG-21, but if I could use a Sparrow in the intercept, the choice might be different."

"Would you return to combat, and did you know the North Vietnamese had placed a bounty on your head?" I answered yes to both.

On the whole, the interview was suprisingly painless. It was good to get some of my feelings into the public domain. Months later one of our returning POWs told me that the North Vietnamese had pictures of Willie and me taken during this interview — guess they wanted to get positive identification for the local bounty hunters!

After the conference we were debriefed and told to expect an award from President Thieu. He never took the time out of his schedule to see us.

That evening we were escorted by Air Force and Navy brass to the Tan Son Nhut Officers' Club in a black limousine. We prepared ourselves for a dull, uneventful dinner complete with endless questions. After dinner the club was relatively quiet with a few Air Force officers milling around, so we retired to the bar. Irish decided to hit the sack early.

About an hour later I heard bursts of yelling and cheering from the main dining room. In minutes the place had filled to capacity with what seemed like 10,000 guys jammed into one room watching a troop of Australian performers. There wasn't anything too exciting except for the three beautiful round-eyed girls singing and dancing in long dresses. The admiral got us a table right up front. Yep, the girls were good looking, but W.C. Fields could have carried a better tune.

We soon found out why the troop was so popular. A banjo player started picking up the tempo as one of the girls threw a glove to the staring boys in blue. Next came the shoes, and finally we beheld some of the most gorgeous female anatomy I had seen in some time. For the moment I almost wished I had joined the Air Force, but my better judgment prevailed.

After the show had progressed for about 20 minutes, someone walked up to the band leader and handed him a piece of paper. The girls stopped, to the deafening jeers of the audience. No one could figure out what was going on as a general made his way to the microphone onstage. One guy near me said, "It must be pretty bad to stop our show."

The Air Force general asked for quiet, "Gents, Lieutenant Randy Cunningham is in the room tonight."

"Who the hell is that?" came out from the mass of people, and pandemonium set in again. The general waited for the clamor to die down, then continued, "We are honored tonight by the presence of Lieutenant Cunningham. Yesterday he shot down three North Vietnamese MiGs, bringing his total to five, making him the first ace of the war. Lieutenant Cunningham was also shot down by a surface-to-air missile while exiting the Red River Valley."

The room exploded as the troops went absolutely wild! Beer cans went sailing across the room, guys jumped up and down on tables and a cheer went up that stunned the senses. It seemed everyone saw the white Navy uniform at once — I was grabbed, hoisted high up in the air and passed around the room on a sea of hands. The jostle was

Press interviews were sometimes more difficult for me than combat. Here Willie and I answer questions during our first media event after becoming aces, in Saigon.

hurting my back, but the emotional high far outweighed the pain.

Bruised and feeling like I had been thrown into a washing machine, I was placed on center stage. The sea of Air Force, Navy, Marine Corps and Army officers stood in a five-minute ovation. I was at a total loss as to how to respond, so I took the mike and told these guys I was ready to continue the anatomy lesson. A loud voice out of the group bellowed, "You can bet your ass on that, Navy!" With that, I made the highlight of the trip by introducing the next stripper.

I think every officer in the place came over and offered to buy a drink. Several American service women joined us to round out the evening. My back was killing me and I was dog tired, so I finally slipped away to get some sleep.

The next day we made a TV tape and took a ride through Saigon. I had always pictured the city as a dirty mud hole, but it turned out to be one of the cleanest, prettiest cities I had ever seen, though the barbed wire didn't help the view.

This was about all the sightseeing we got to do. Our two-day stay in Saigon was crammed with more TV interviews and debriefs before hitching the mail plane back out to our "fighting lady."

We came back aboard in the midst of getting an air strike off. The tempo aboard ship, if anything, had increased, so our arrival was barely noticed by the hard-working flight deck crews.

Irish and I headed for the para-rigger's shop to be fitted with new flight gear... the old stuff was a bit salty. I had just been stuffed into a new G suit when Commander Newman walked in. "Duke, turn in your flight gear. You're going home tomorrow."

Most guys would have been overjoyed, but I no longer had a wife and child to return to. I could go to my parents', but I had no desire to face anyone, with my broken heart.

I tried everything to rescind the order. MiGs were flying after years of inactivity — why leave the hunt when game was plentiful? Manfred von Richthofen had 75 more kills in him when he had reached my point, and I didn't want to wait 20 years for another war. I was told that I had other things valuable to the Navy besides flying.

First off, if Irish and I were shot down, we would most likely never see home again. The bounty on our heads was no TV western stuff to Hanoi. That old fear of capture left me without argument. Secondly, if captured, our political value to the enemy would be exploited and

The entire population of my home town turned out to welcome me back as 3,000 folks in Shelbina, Missouri took in the parade. My son Todd rode with me.

the Navy would rather get some mileage out of us Stateside.

This saying good-bye to the guys was getting old. After making the rounds on ship we went topside to face the congregation of *Connie's* men. T.T. Tyler, backed by a group of troopers, presented me with one of the deck crew's yellow jerseys signed by all the men crowded around. I have that jersey hanging in my den, and I wouldn't sell it for a hundred million bucks. The names scribbled on that piece of cloth represent the real effort in the destruction of five MiGs.

The C-1 flight over the Gulf to Cubi Point seemed almost endless at 130 knots. When we finally arrived the place was virtually deserted, so we hired a car and drove to Clark AFB. For the first time since I had been in the Navy I didn't have to wait three days for a space-available seat — we left the next morning for Japan.

Both Willie and I were apprehensive about what kind of reception we would receive back in the States. Would the candle burners and the anti-war groups mob us? Would there be ticker tape parades or egg throwers? Irish slept most of the way back, but I spent most of the time fighting back tears while wondering what was left of my marriage.

After we touched down in Los Angeles everything shifted into high gear. We were quickly escorted to a small plane where Navy aides waited to brief and assist us for the coming interviews. A short hop to San Diego and we boarded black limousines waiting to take us to the main entrance, where a large group of people were gathered waving signs: "Bless the Blockade and our two Aces." There were 200 wives of men on *Connie* to greet us. At midnight!

The lights were so bright I could only make out figures at first. I broke up completely at the sight of my wife and son. All I wanted to do was to hold Susie and Todd.

Vice Admiral Walker, Commander Naval Air Forces, U.S. Pacific Fleet, welcomed us home and asked us to say something. I have no idea what came out of my mouth — the warm reception so late at night was an unexpected treat — but I was wrapped up in the mixed emotions of seeing my broken family.

A two-week publicity tour of the United States had been laid on (it eventually stretched out to five months.) Susie accompanied me on the first leg, but the marriage was over. She had written my parents and told them about it all, and she confessed she only stuck around to

The new generation of American aces. Cunningham and Driscoll (left and right) with Steve Ritchie and Chuck DeBellevue, the Air Force ace team in Vietnam. This meeting occurred at the reunion of the American Fighter Aces Association in San Antonio during 1972.

pick up the excitement of the event. She was meeting with a guy only a block away from our home. It was more than I could take, so we filed for divorce. This was going on while I was supposedly the happy ace touring the country. Irish, knowing how my insides were being torn apart, helped me as no one else could.

During those five months I received thousands of cards and letters lauding our efforts and accomplishments. I found but one adverse note. There were no ticker tape parades, no large crowds gathered to honor us as they did the POWs, but I did appreciate the small civilian and military groups full of questions and appreciation. Walking down the streets of New York was a joy — people who recognized us from the *Today* TV show stopped their cars, jumped out and shook our hands.

In Denver, during a Flag Day celebration and parade, an antiwar group picketed the ceremony, requesting I talk with them. Hesitant at first, I finally agreed and found myself in a very stimulating exchange of ideas.

When we stopped in St. Louis to visit the McDonnell-Douglas plant, makers of the Phantom, my parents were beaming as I climbed from the airplane. I needed them more than ever, and I was overjoyed that they had driven up from Shelbina. The whole family had been close — I seem to remember that Mom and Dad never missed a ball game that my brother Bob or I played in. They often sacrificed much personally to see us kids make it. A piece of Dad's advice stuck with me through much of my personal ordeal, both in combat and back home: "Son, if you fear something, you have to beat that fear, making yourself just a little more of a man."

And I did get to ride in a parade after all! When we got to Shelbina, the whole town of 3,000 people turned out and this small, sleepy farming community held its first parade for Randall, Jr. My heart warmed at the recognition from people I had grown up with. It was a tonic, and I enjoyed every minute. Yet the war had touched this town also. One of my best friends was missing, Lieutenant Ronald Cullers, a classmate who had been killed in Vietnam. My second home was the Cullers' house. I was both saddened and warmed to see Ron's parents again.

The five months of touring became one endless roast beef dinner after the other. Breakfast, lunch and dinner — I think the astronauts called this glad-handing public relations stuff "being in the barrel."

EJECTION SEAT

RESCUE

1. PUSH BUTTON C OPEN DOOR
2. SQUEEZE "T" HANDLE AND PULL
TO JETTISON CANOPY

Mounting up for my
first flight in an
F-14 Tomcat.

Irish and I averaged three cities a day with two or three media interviews in each. By the end, my life was running out of steam. I had no inner reserves to draw on, and this being an ace did not fill the void.

As is typical with most prayers prayed in dire circumstances, I failed my first promise to the Lord. I don't imagine He was too pleased with the next year of my life as I let everything go. Nothing mattered anymore except my son, Todd. Sure, I had gotten back into flying fighters, but without some kind of inner strength to support me, it held no sustaining power for my battered state.

When I thought I had hit rock-bottom, a man named Dan McKinnon introduced himself to me. Dan is the kind of person who instinctively knows what needs to be done in tough situations. His concern awakened in me a desire to pull out of my spin.

Wasting no time, Dan invited me to attend church with him the next Sunday — I frankly told him it would be a waste of both his and my time, the way I felt. He simply smiled and asked me over to the house for dinner, undaunted. I thought I had nothing to lose and accepted.

Upon arriving I saw that Dan had stacked the deck... couldn't get me to church, so he invited over some Christian friends. I was introduced to Hal Lindsey and his wife, Jan. Before too long, it was obvious Hal had something on the ball. As the author of such books as *The Late, Great Planet Earth*; *Satan Is Alive And Well On Planet Earth* and *There Is A New World Coming*, he had more than a passing knowledge about the claims of Jesus Christ.

Taking a special interest in me, Hal cast aside his busy schedule to bring one lost pilot to God. There had been a long stretch of time since my promise to find Jesus was made in a rolling, bucking, burning Phantom, but there I was face to face with the presence of God. I asked the Lord to come into my life and take over. I had run things so far and it was a total mess. There was certainly no doubt about the sin question — I had done enough of that.

The forgiveness was complete as He washed me inside. Sure, the problems didn't go away, but the Spirit of God had entered me to run the show. And being a new Christian wasn't easy, either. Dan, Hal and Jan never left me alone to flounder around. They always encouraged me to face things with the Lordship of Christ in mind, rather than selfish ambition.

That was tough for an ego-centered guy like me. But it had been tough for another guy Dan introduced to me — Johnny Cash. Wow, had *he* been through some rough times before he finally made peace with God and himself. As successful as he had become, he lost it all to a raunchy life, then regained it and more with God in control. Johnny made it clear to me that had it not been for his wife, June Carter, he would have given up. June held the fort and finally led her man in black to the Lord.

These three couples had much to do with my keeping that promise to God. As a result, my life has meaning again; much more than it had before.

But as personal problems arise and are solved, the global situation seems perenially troubled. The United States, in my estimation, faces its toughest tests in the future. For the first time, our military and moral strength has begun to crack under the strain of the mightiest weapons build-up in the history of mankind, as the Soviet Union continues to challenge freedom. And our lack of moral and spiritual strength at home — first evidenced during the Vietnam War — endangers a resolve to stand firm in the face of this totalitarian onslaught.

As I've said, I was born on December 8, 1941. Yet the pre-Pearl Harbor mentality of the 1930s which left the free world doomed to six years of global war is again being voiced. We are somehow expected to reach accommodation with our sworn enemies without maintaining the ability to defend ourselves against their demonstrated penchant for aggression.

In 1974 I married Nancy Jones, and we have two beautiful daughters, making my life complete. God willing, my grandchildren will not see war.

Yet, it could happen again. Only next time the stakes will be much higher.

APPENDIX A
THE AIR COMBAT ARENA

The last MiG of the war was downed on 12 January 1973 by Lieutenant Vic Kovaleski teamed with Lieutenant Jim Wise as RIO in an old F-4B from VF-161 of *Midway*. What a year it had been! I only wish I had the space to record every MiG kill from the first, a 17 downed by Commander Louis Page and Lieutenant John C. Smith on 17 June 1965. Ironically, they flew an F-4B from *Midway*, too.

The war in Southeast Asia produced two "ace crews" and another back-seater with five MiG kills while flying with different pilots:

Lt. Randall Cunningham and Lt(jg) William Driscoll USN	5
Capt. Richard S. Ritchie and	
Capt. Charles B. DeBellevue (6)	USAF 5
Capt. Jeffrey S. Feinstein, WSO	USAF 5

To say that I am proud to be numbered among them is an understatement.

But despite all the glory and excitement, those of us who killed MiGs experienced a larger disappointment in the air-to-air arena. During the 1965-68 period, the Navy's kill-to-loss ratio was 2.42 to 1 while the Air Force came out slightly behind with 2.25 to 1. This simply means we barely managed to down two MiGs for every fighter we lost — totally unacceptable. During the second major air combat period, in 1972, the Navy's kill ratio soared to 12.0 to 1 while the Air Force dropped to 1.88 to 1.

There were very clear reasons for this disparity.

Through the end of the Korean War and a bit beyond, air combat maneuvering (formerly dogfighting, hasseling, red-dogging) was as much a part of fighter pilot training as the guns mounted in the aircraft. In the late 1950s, however, the concept evolved in western air forces that missiles would replace guns in aerial combat.

This was due primarily to the changing ideas of warfare in the nuclear age. The next war was expected to be fought with ICBMs and long-range bombers. The projected need in fighter aircraft would, therefore, be a fast, high-flying interceptor armed with long-range missiles and sophisticated radar. The enemy would be hunted on the scope and the pilot would never see the target aircraft. Thus were born the ideas which produced the F-4 Phantom II, the F-106 Delta Dart and other fighter-interceptors of the era.

The Vought F-8 Crusader, an excellent air-superiority fighter, would be succeeded in the Navy by the "miracle" F-4 that would (presumably) eliminate the need for air combat maneuvering. The Air Force was building its fighter force around the F-105 nuclear bomber, which doubled as a tactical aircraft. In the Navy, F-8 pilots formed the small cadre of dedicated air combat thinkers as the F-4 took over the fleet. Later this showed up marvelously in Vietnam: when everyone else was getting shot out of the sky, the F-8 drivers got 18 MiGs confirmed for the loss of three during 1965-1968!

The first American air offensive over North Vietnam, Operating Rolling Thunder, was a painful slap in the face to both the U.S. Navy and Air Force. From 1965 through 1968, 110 MiGs were shot down in aerial engagements. We lost 48 fighters for a kill-loss ratio of 2.29 to 1 overall. Compared to the Korean War's 10 to 1, it was a disaster.

The close-in, visual maneuvering air battle had rudely returned. The "shoot without seeing" technique using missiles designed to hit non-maneuvering targets was painfuly inadequate. Since the F-4 was earmarked as a fleet defense fighter, the pilot was not allowed to pull more than three Gs — the radar was susceptible to "breaking the lock" under high G loads. As a result, the F-8s were put in to fight the MiGs, but the Crusaders were getting old. They began to stand down due to airframe stress, and though they flew all through the war, the Navy began to launch F-4s as air superiority fighters.

By mid-1968 the Navy had ordered a report to be made on what was lacking in fighter doctrine based upon egagements occurring between July and November 1968. Captain Frank W. Ault's report uncovered the basic fact that pilots were not being trained for the classic maneuvering battle. Not being worried about promotion, Frank laid it on the line to the "stone age" mentality: "In the past we may have concentrated too extensively on improving the machine without spending enough effort on the man who flies the aircraft."

By September 1968 the fledgling Navy Fighter Weapons School was established at NAS Miramar near San Diego. Thus was born "Top Gun." A-4 Skyhawks became MiG-17s and F-8s duplicated MiG-21s. Air Force F-106s, also excellent MiG-21 simulators, were later flown in the program through a 1970 agreement between the Navy and the Aerospace Defense Command. The following year the Navy's Atlantic Fleet aggressor squadron, VF-43, was flying A-4s out of NAS Oceana, Virginia.

The first Top Gun graduates were in fleet squadrons by April 1969. The Navy's foresight paid off during the Linebacker operations over the North in 1972; the average kills per engagement soared from 0.20 to 1.04. When I went into combat I had over 200 simulated dogfights behind me.

By way of comparison, in DaNang I met an Air Force C-130 transport pilot who had just transitioned to F-4s. He went through a total of 12 air combat training flights, then he was going up North to fight MiGs! I considered this situation an out-and-out crime.

The USAF's first dissimilar air combat tactics (DACT) program was initiated in 1967 by the Aerospace Defense Command (ADC). Up to this point (and for some time afterwards) most air combat training was against an aircraft of the same type, the only variable being pilot ability. The first instructors were trained at the USAF Fighter Weapons School at Nellis AFB, Nevada. F-106s were flown against F-4s and F-100s.

In 1968 the ADC program was transferred to the USAF Interceptor Weapons School at Tyndall AFB, Florida, now called College Dart. After the 1970 Navy-ADC agreement, the first joint service training exercise was conducted at Miramar between Air Force 84th Fighter-Interceptor Squadron F-106s and Navy VF-121 Phantoms.

The USAF found the air combat situation in Vietnam harder to solve. Tactical Air Comand F-4s flew close air support, interdiction and air superiority while more Navy F-4s were freed for the air superiority mission by the A-4s, A-6s and A-7s. The Air Force's own Red Baron Report on MiG encounters cited "insufficient training and experience in air-to-air combat." Specifically: training had been conducted against similar aircraft also employing USAF tactics combined with inadequate command and control; an average visual acquisition range for the smaller MiGs was only 1.6 nautical miles (well within Atoll heat-seeking parameters); and F-4 UHF communications problems and poor radio discipline further complicated matters.

During the Air Force's airwar over North Vietnam, 65 percent of its Sparrows and 45 percent of its Sidewidners malfunctioned due to launch, guidance or fuzing failures. The Navy had a rough time, too, as previously related. Added to this hardware problem were missiles fired out of parameters. Of the 204 Sparrows which functioned properly, 55 percent were fired outside required launch zones. Of 245 Sidewinders, half were not fired within lethal parameters.

Twenty-eight of the kills achieved against Air Force planes were by a totally undetected enemy. Of six Navy F-4s lost to MiGs, only one was downed in a dogfight — the others were shot down from the rear, never knowing MiGs were behind. Even when MiGs were detected, crucial errors were made in visual range estimates, a small aircraft appearing to the *untrained* eye to be at greater then actual range. Add to that the lack of flying against enemy tactics in training, and you have a real can of worms. One can appreciate my facetious remark to the Air Force colonel in Da Nang who wanted to know how to improve the Air Force kill ratio.

On the whole, the Air Force used the Sparrow more than the Navy. We operated east of Hanoi, facing a cluttered threat area, therefore risking a shot at a friendly aircraft if we launched a Sparrow by radar alone. Even so, several of our guys had to avoid Sparrows coming out of nowhere! The Air Force even shot down a couple of its own. Hence the importance of visual identification.

During the combats of 1972 the Navy shot down 23 of its 24 MiGs with Sidewinders. The Air Force used the Sparrow more due to firm radar identification of bandits from their ground radar sites, whereas our Red Crown control ships had a harder time determining much more than bogies on their scopes. A bogey could turn out to be a friendly or a bandit.

Before Linebacker was over, TAC formed the 64th Fighter Weapons Squadron at Nellis in October 1972, flying T-38s as aggressors. For the first time in 20 years the United States had a realistic air combat training program set up for the fighter pilots of all three services.

The major argument against ACM or ACT training has been

safety. Aggressively maneuvering two or more large, expensive fighting machines in the same airspace can be dangerous, but the programs seem to upgrade pilot skills to the point of almost eliminating accidents. The F-4 accident rate in the Navy is 2.77 per 10,000 flying hours — only .172 are due to ACM. More important, though, is the exposure of Navy and Air Force fighter pilots to every type of proposed threat in a controlled situation.

When we go play Red Baron on each other, the ground rules call for a "deck" altitude of 5,000-feet, trying not to go below 10,000 if possible. An imaginary 500- to 1,000-foot bubble surrounds each fighter, and no one is allowed to penetrate it. This does cramp realism a bit, since most Navy MiG kills took place below 5,000 feet, many below 500, and we often passed other aircraft by mere feet. Regardless, these rules help keep us safe.

Each mission is always prebriefed, face to face, to discuss rules of engagement, emergency procedures, when to break off a fight and other safety factors. The days of "let's go and have at it" are gone.

The missions are carefully monitored. The advent of air combat maneuvering ranges provides a taped computer readout of each aircraft's maneuvers — no guesswork when back on the ground as to who won. The radar controllers who work with both the Navy and Air Force aggressor squadrons have been thoroughly schooled in Soviet intercept tactics.

The aggressor pilots have over 1,000 hours of fighter time with a wide variety of air-to-air experience. Continually required to fly as Soviet fighter pilots would, they give American aviators very realistic training. The aircraft are even painted in known Communist Bloc color schemes, complete with red two-digit numbers on the nose.

The F-5E Tiger II is the prominent MiG simulator in both the Navy and Air Force. The F-5 has a fine turn rate and is capable of Mach 1.6, close to the 1.9 of the MiG-21. It also has a gunsight and weapons that make it just like the real thing.

As if to confirm all the effort we are once more putting into ACM, the statistics from the 1973 Yom Kippur War in the Middle East present an excellent example. The Israeli Air Force was unable to eliminate Arab air power as it had in 1967 due to bomb-proof shelters and a remarkably effective use of AAA and SAMs. The systems were all Soviet-built. The Israelis were forced to achieve aerial superiority through air-to-air combat as a result of this massive anti-aircraft network. Should hostilities break out in Central Europe, NATO will have to attain air superiority in the same way, against the even better Warsaw Pact defenses. I am firmly convinced that realistic training will do much to offset the Soviet advantage.

Less than seven of the 335 kills achieved by the Israelis in 1973 were made with Sparrows from beyond visual range. The remainder of the kills were obtained by heat-seeking Sidewinder and Shafrir missiles, or cannon within visual range during maneuvering engagements. It still comes down to a dogfight. And the same has held true during more recent air battles over Lebanon, the Falklands and the Mediterranean through 1982.

Ten years ago the three services — USAF, USN, USMC — were locked into their own worlds, coping with air combat training as best they could with what in-house resources were available. Now each service's fighter pilots are fully involved in joint ACM-ACT training on a regular basis. For the past few years an Annual Joint Interservice Dissimilar Air Combat Training Conference has been held at the Pentagon to co-ordinate resources for maximized efficiency, training and budget savings.

I have to say that Navy pilots are the best! (I have nothing against the Air Force boys, I just wouldn't want my daughter to marry one.) But interservice rivalry (based upon justifiable pride) takes a back seat when fighter pilots congregate with one goal in mind — be the best at all times when faced with the possibility of engaging a common enemy. When one service wishes to contact another to "fight," a phone is picked up which links eight Air Force bases, 26 Naval facilities or 15 Marine points of contact. It's that simple to get the training.

This revolution in air combat training, brought about by the harsh lessons of Southeast Asia, has resulted in some major doctrinal changes and the reinforcing of older concepts that have proven the test of time.

The most significant change in fighter flying has been the introduction of the "loose deuce" formation — the Air Force calls it tactical partnership. The "welded wing" flying of the past is gone, ending wingman subserviance and the "cone of darkness" or lack of visibility behind aircraft flying in close formation. The old "finger four" (pioneered by the Luftwaffe) doesn't find many adherants now.

The loose deuce formation is flown in lateral separation, spread one to two nautical miles apart with 3,000 to 5,000 feet vertical separation. An intrusion by an attacker requires only a break in one direction or the other to sandwich the single attacker. No time is wasted in first splitting, then breaking. Any turn or maneuver must be out of the line of bearing, lest both aircraft be sighted by the enemy. It is also more difficult to attack a vertically split formation.

The great simplicity is that this defensive-patrol formation is also the best possible offensive formation. Since each aircraft can easily clear the other's tail, they could potentially fight several adversaries as each checks the other's six o'clock. Both aircraft are effective fighters, whereas the Fluid Four essentially cuts combat effectiveness by 50 percent, limiting the wingman to sticking to his leader at all times and compromising his offensive potential. In the tactical partnership, each aircraft can alternate between free fighter and engaged fighter. The free fighter can look over the situation by sitting up high, pulling the engaged partner out of tight spots when necessary. An adversary usually concentrates on the engaged fighter — watching two can be rough. And in these days of expensive aircraft, all resources are maximized for optimum availability.

A tactical storm still brews concerning single-seat versus two-seat fighters. There can be no question that Willie's pair of eyeballs in my F-4 pulled me out of some tight corners. The Navy continues the two-seat line of thinking in the F-14 but the Air Force is going back to single-seaters in the F-15 and F-16, and the Navy and Marines are doing likewise with the F-18. This worries some of my buddies who have experienced the added value of another ACM-trained crewman aboard. On the other hand, an extra man plus the equipment he needs add a great deal of weight to the aircraft and cuts into its performance. The F-15 overcomes much of the technical complexity normally handled by two people in placing simplified systems controls within easy reach of the pilot, allowing him to remain "heads up," seated high in the bubble canopy. The doctrinal differences have yet to be resolved in both services.

Thankfully, guns are back in the aircraft — every new-generation fighter has an internal 20- or 30mm cannon. As I said earlier, had I possessed a gun during my tour in Southeast Asia I am sure I could have downed several more MiGs.

Paint is also getting a more realistic consideration in aerial combat. The "lizard" color scheme Air Force planes were fine when down in the weeds, but during aerial combat they stood out as almost black against haze, clouds or sky. Presently, light blue and gray shading is finding its way onto fighters to render them less visible. The fighter pilot dictum "He who sees first, lives longest" perfectly fits painting aircraft to match their environment — the sky.

Things have changed surprisingly little since 1915 when Germany's Oswald Boelcke formulated his basis dicta for air fighting. Fighter combat is too fluid to pin down a pilot to specific tactics and doctrines, for that very closed-mindedness led to disaster over North Vietnam, as proven by reduced kill ratios. Boelcke's general guidelines emphasizing speed, surprise, use of altitude and sun remain a better yardstick. For the fighter pilot must be free to propose improvements or he will get himself killed.

Secondly, a fighter pilot must learn all that he can about the enemy's capabilities in men and machines, then go out and fly "combat" against simulated threats. Both the Navy and Air Force reports from Vietnam uncovered inadequate training.

Pappy Boyington put it straight when he said, "The air battle is not necessarily won at the time of the battle. The winner may have been determined by the amount of time, energy, thought and training an individual has previously accomplished in an effort to increase his ability as a fighter pilot."

What does it come down to? Top Gun said it best: YOU FIGHT LIKE YOU TRAIN.

APPENDIX B
THE NORTH VIETNAMESE AIR FORCE

On the whole, the NVAF proved inadequate despite the kill ratios its pilots racked up against us. There were a number of reasons for this.

First of all, their training was too regimented. Every flight was canned and mechanical, leaving little room for pilot initiative. During dogfights it was generally easy to predict what a North Vietnamese pilot was going to do, giving us the advantage. Of course, the exception to the rule almost got me on May 10th. Remember, nothing about tactics is forever true and unchanging.

Also, they — like us — had been exposed to very little ACM. The high-speed intercept, shoot-and-scoot tactic, closely controlled by GCI, was prevalent. And to the North Vietnamese pilot the GCI's word was law. When we jammed enemy radio frequencies, NVAF pilots often became confused, incapable of making a decision on their own. They would often try various tactics and use them until an aircraft was lost. Then they were ordered to discontinue it. This practice must have been confusing for them, to say the least.

The North's pilots were also severely limited on flying time, possibly due to fuel shortages. I know that when intelligence reported a new fuel shipment from China, the MiGs really came up in force. At other times the average Gomer was lucky to get ten hours a month.

The North Vietnamese could have made us pay a higher price for bombing their country if they had pressed for air superiority. As it was, the appearance of the NVAF was sporadic with little forethought as to a wider objective. Apparently they were relying on the ground forces to get the job done. Our large bombers were certainly vulnerable enough, but the MiGs failed to react significantly. In

1972 not one Navy attack aircraft was lost to enemy aircraft.

In late 1972 an Air Force pilot who had been downed by a MiG spent over 20 days on the ground a few miles from Yen Bai, northwest of Hanoi. The MiGs would work hard in simulated whirling, rolling dogfights. They developed low-level tactics to avoid our radars. The 21s would launch after simulated bogies and return to CAP over dogfighting 17s and 19s. Clearly, they were learning as the war drew to a close, but the pilots were still generally of poor caliber without inspired leadership in the air.

Hanoi also had to draw from untested Russian advisors rather than internal, experienced tacticians. The Russians, in my opinion, had outdated tactical doctrines. I think this was borne out by the conflicts in the Middle East. Israeli pilots chewed the Arabs to pieces for many of the same reasons.

This is not to say, by any means, that it was easy. The North had a highly-developed search radar warning system that revealed our every move. Their GCI made it virtually impossible for us to sneak up on the MiGs.

Their airfields were numerous and scattered, launching aircraft that were rugged and versatile, requiring less maintenance than their American counterparts. And boy, could the North ever hide 'em on the ground. Caves in the karst ranges, revetted concrete bunkers and super camouflage in storage areas. If we cratered the runways with 1,000-pound bombs, the relentless workers had them operational again in a few hours. It was a tough proposition to get at the North's airpower on the ground.

North Vietnam's ground and air co-ordination was superb. We would enter a target area and get everything thrown at us — SAMs, AAA, smallarms fire, slingshots! Let a MiG appear and all ground fire would cease until the MiGs retired. Then the band would strike up again.

The NVAF operated in a small tactical area with the whopping advantage of sanctuary in China. If a Gomer was lucky enough to survive a shootdown, he would be having a beer in the officers' club while our downed pilots could expect pumpkin soup for the evening meal.

Certainly, the strong points of the MiGs themselves have been evident throughout this volume. The MiG-17 was the star of the NVAF due to its ability to turn on a dime. The better Arab pilots in the Middle East preferred to fly it. It had good guns, the 37mm and

23mm cannon, and two Atolls. As seen previously, enough of us learned about these points the hard way.

The 17 was limited to subsonic speeds, possessing a roll rate of only 136° per second. The pilot was also limited by non-boosted flight controls. Yet if an F-8 or F-4 slowed below 450 knots, the 17 driver definitely had the advantage.

I am surprised we didn't see more of the MiG-19. It had a phenomenal turn and roll rate and it could accelerate with the F-4 right up to 400 knots, when the Phantom began to pull away. Yet the 19 had only 3,800 pounds of fuel, giving it very poor range. All three MiG types had poor range, for that matter.

The MiG-21 remains the dominant Russian-built fighter of the 1960s and 1970s, and it will be around for awhile, as will the F-4, even though East and West are building better, more capable fighters. Above 20,000 feet the 21 had certain advantages over the Phantom due to the latter's high wing loading. But the F-4 had two 18,000-pound thrust engines to push it out of tight spots, and a better missile system.

At lower altitudes the F-4 could handle the 21, the winner being decided by pilot ability. But again, if the Phantom got slow it was in trouble. During 1972, MiG-21s accounted for 23 of the 29 American fighters lost in aerial combat. While this may reflect the larger number of 21s in the NVAF inventory, the 21 usually wasn't a lot of trouble since it was relegated to the tactic of shooting an Atoll and running. During 1972 no American aircraft were lost to the 21's guns. For that matter, I don't recall anyone being shot at by a 21 cannoneer.

All three MiGs had poor rearward visibility. Our most effective kill position was within 30° of dead six. Often MiG drivers never knew what hit them — it works both ways!

When the stops were finally pulled in 1972, the United States forced the North to cease hostilities through airpower alone. There were no invading troops, no beach-heads. This was the first time in history that a war had been brought to an end solely by action from the air.

Our own politicians tied our hands for so long that I have no doubt we could have gotten it done in 1965. Yet every time the "Yankee Imperialists" opened a telling wound up North, the outraged screams would cause Congress to limit us. This still seems incredible to me, but finally we saw the thing ended. Only history can judge the rights and wrongs of the Vietnam era. Militarily, though, the lessons were harsh and clear. I only pray we will not have to relearn them in the future.

APPENDIX C
GLOSSARY

AAA   Anti-Aircraft Artillery, also Triple A.

ACM   Air Combat Maneuvering, or dogfighting. the
                 Air Force term is ACT, for Air Combat Tactics.

ACMR   Air Combat Maneuvering Range. A highly-
                 instrumented practice area.

AGL   Above Ground Level. I.E., height above the
                 ground.

Air-to-Ground Normally refers to gunnery or bombing from
                 aircraft against surface targets. The fighter
                 community jokingly calls this "air-to-mud" or
                 "moving dirt."

Angle-Off   The angle between the longitudinal axis of a
                 defender and the line of sight of an attacker.

Aspect Angle   The angle between a bogey's flight path and the
                 line of sight to an interceptor.

Atoll   An infrared heat-seeking air-to-air missile fired
                 by Soviet-built fighters. Similar to our AIM-9B
                 Sidewinder.

Bandit   An aircraft identified as hostile. Over North
                 Vietnam, bandits were color-coded. Red was a

MiG-17, White a MiG-19 and Blue a MiG-21.

Bogey
An approaching aircraft not yet identified as friend or foe. Usually assumed to be hostile until proven otherwise.

Bolter
Failure to engage the arresting cable while landing on an aircraft carrier. Usually due to failure to lower the arresting hook.

Break
A maneuver or command to initiate a maximum-rate turn to avoid an attacking aircraft or to defeat a tracking missile.

Burner
Slang term for jet engine's afterburner.

Buster
Full military power; 100 percent of engine power without afterburner.

CAG
Carrier Air Group Commander. The term is left over from WW II, since aircraft carrier units are now designated air wings rather than air groups.

CAP
Combat Air Patrol. There are different types of CAPs:
BARCAP: Normally two fighters positioned between threat aircraft and an aircraft carrier. Short for Barrier Combat Air Patrol.
FORCECAP: Normally a section of two fighters positioned to intercept any airborne threat to a strike force of bombers.
MIGCAP: A section of fighters free to intercept any airborne threat, with the primary mission of killing the threat aircraft.
RESCAP: A section or more of fighters positioned to provide both air and ground protection to the rescue of a downed flier.
TARCAP: A section of fighters positioned near

an airborne strike force for its protection to and from the target. The primary mission is discouraging rather than killing threat aircraft.

Clock Positions   Calls relative to things outside an aircraft are made as if the nose were 12 o'clock, the tail 6 o'clock, the right wing 3 o'clock and the left wing 9 o'clock.

COD   Carrier Onboard Delivery aircraft, usually bringing mail to an aircraft carrier or serving as a ship-to-shore shuttle.

DMZ   Demilitarized Zone. An ironic term when applied to Vietnam, as it denoted the border between North and South.

ECM   Electronic Counter-Measures. Jamming or otherwise confusing enemy radio and radar frequencies, usually from specialized aircraft.

Effective Range   The maximum distance at which a weapon may be expected to hit the target or inflict damage. Always less than maximum range, which is merely the ultimate distance the weapon will carry, regardless of accuracy.

FAC   Forward Air Controller, either airborne or on the ground. He co-ordinates attacking aircraft around a chosen target.

Feet Dry   A call to indicate that an aircraft has crossed the shore and is over land instead of water.

Flak Suppression   A counter-defense mission involving two or more fighters armed with bombs and air-to-air missiles. They are to attack AAA or SAM sites which may threaten a strike group. After hitting the targets and expending air-ground ordnance they become FORCECAP fighters.

Fox One or Two	Radio call indicating launch of a Sparrow (Fox One) or Sidewinder (Two).
GCI	Ground-Controlled Intercept, in which a radar station directs an airborne fighter to an interception.
Gomers	Slang term employed to identify the North Vietnamese.
Helo	Slang term for helicopter.
Jinking	Continuous random change of aircraft heading and altitude to negate enemy tracking.
MiG	Loosely applied, an appelation for all Soviet-built fighter-bombers. Actually it stands for the Soviet design team of Mikoyan-Gurevich which has produced the leading Russian fighters beginning with the MiG-1 of 1941. The designation is frequently misspelled in all capital letters but actually reflects the Mi of Artem I. Mikoyan and the G of Mikhail I. Gurevich.
NAS	Naval Air Station.
NFO	Naval Flight Officer. Commissioned aircrew member other than a pilot.
No Joy	No visual contact.
Nugget	A new flight-crew member, denoting little experience.
Overshoot	Occurs when an aircraft passes in front of another due to an excessive closure rate from behind. In fighter combat an overshoot places

the faster aircraft in a vulnerable position.

Punch Out	Bail-out from a jet aircraft by ejection seat.
RIO	Radar Intercept Officer, the Naval Flight Officer who occupies the back seat of F-4s and F-14s. The Air Force term is WSO, of Weapons System Officer.
ROE	Rules of Engagement; the specific guidelines under which fighters may engage opposing aircraft. Also applies to policies and targeting for bombers.
SAM	Surface-to-Air Missile.
SAR	Search-and-Rescue.
SEA	Southeast Asia.
Sidewinder	The AIM-9 air-to-air intercept missile. It requires an infrared heat source to track, notably the heat generated by a target aircraft's engine. The greater the heat source, the more effectively the missile tracks. An afterburning engine is the ideal target.
Sparrow	The AIM-7 air-to-air intercept missile. Though initially designed for the interceptor role in fleet defense, AIM-7 has been modified to give it a low-altitude dogfight capability. It is used in conjunction with the F-4's radar system, requiring a radar lock onto target for firing. The missile follows the lock-on returns to the target through all weather conditions.
Tally-Ho	A radio call indicating visual contact with a bandit. The term originated in the Royal Air Force as an affectation of hunting terminology.

Top Gun	The U.S. Navy Fighter Weapons School at NAS Miramar, California, responsible for ACM training for fleet fighter pilots.
Unload	To place an aircraft in zero G for maximum acceleration.
Yo-Yo	A vertical combat maneuver.
XO	Executive Officer, second-in-command of a squadron or ship.

APPENDIX D
AIRCRAFT

A-3   The Douglas Skywarrior, a large twin-engine aircraft ori-
        ginally designed for heavy attack. Though subsonic, it
        possesses tremendous range and endurance. It was employed
        in two special mission roles in Vietnam: as an aerial tanker
        for refueling other aircraft (KA-3) and as an ECM bird
        (EA-3). The A-3's size earned it the affectionate nickname
        "Whale," and EA-3s were sometimes called "Electric
        Whales."

A-5   The Vigilante was a sensationally fast strike aircraft when it
        joined the fleet. Capable of nearly Mach Two, it was intended
        as a nuclear bomber but was almost wholly employed as a
        very fast two-seat tactical reconnaissance aircraft. "Vigie"
        drivers are still known for their sky-high morale, even
        though the type has been withdrawn from service. The recce
        birds are called RA-5s.

A-6   Grumman's Intruder was the most advanced all-weather
        strike aircraft in the world when it entered combat in 1965.
        The crew of pilot and navigator-bombardier sit side-by-side,
        employing some of the most sophisticated avionics equipment
        ever installed in a tactical aircraft. The A-6 packs as much
        ordnance externally as a B-17 of WW II, and though subsonic
        it can bomb accurately in any weather, day or night. The
        ECM version is actually a different aircraft, as the EA-6B is
        lengthened to accommodate three electronics warfare oper-
        ators in the Prowler.

A-7   Officially the Corsair II after the Vought company's famous gull-wing F4U of WW II fame, the A-7 was flown by both the Navy and Air Force. It entered combat in 1967 as a single-seat attack aircraft capable of greater speed and payload than the smaller Douglas A-4 Skyhawk. Extremely popular, the A-7 has been described by pilots as "a gentleman's airplane." It carried 20mm cannon in addition to bombs and rockets.

C-1   The standard COD aircraft during Vietnam was the C-1 Trader. It was actually a variant of the S-2 Tracker, a twin-engine propeller-driven anti-submarine aircraft. The versatile little C-1 delivered everything which could be stuffed into its fuselage, hauling mail, people and spare parts from shore bases to carriers at sea and back again.

E-2   Grumman's Hawkeye is "the eye of the fleet." As a carrier-based airborne early warning aircraft, it can detect enemy aircraft long before they're visible and direct interceptors to the kill. Powered by two turbo-prop engines, the E-2 has a five-man crew and a 24-foot radar dish mounted atop the fuselage.

F-4   Probably the most famous aircraft of the Vietnam War, the Phantom II was named for McDonnell Aircraft's first jet, the FH-1 of 1946. But the "Phantastic Phantom" far eclipsed the record of any previous military jet. It entered Navy service in 1958 and was adopted by the Air Force in 1962. Acting as a fighter-bomber, the twin-engine, two-seat F-4 performed a variety of other duties including photo-reconnaissance and SAM-killer in the "Wild Weasel" configuration. Air Force Phantoms were armed with 20mm guns during the war, but Navy F-4s retained the mixed Sidewinder-Sparrow armament only. In the bombing role, the F-4 can carry up to 16,000 pounds of ordnance. The most common version in combat during 1971-72 was the F-4J, which was capable of Mach Two.

F-8   "Last of the Gunfighters" is how Crusader pilots described their beloved Vought fighter. Armed with four 20mm cannon in addition to Sidewinders, F-8s shot down at least 18 MiGs while losing only three in aerial combat, for the best kill-loss ratio of the Vietnam War. This speedster was a single-engine, single-seat fighter in the Corsair tradition which proved just as versatile as the F4U. It ended its combat service largely as a carrier-based photo-recon type in the RF-8 model.

OV-10 North American's Bronco came from the same stable as the immortal Mustang of WW II. Distinctive with its twin-engine, twin-boom configuration, the OV-10 was used by the Air Force, Navy and Marines primarily as a spotter aircraft. But one Navy squadron made excellent use of the type as an attack aircraft.

MiG-17 Bearing a distinct family resemblance to the famed MiG-15 of Korean War fame, the 17 appeared in 1953. It has served in more than 20 air forces around the world and was probably the most numerous North Vietnamese fighter through 1968. Primary armament was a mixture of 23mm and 37mm cannon with option for Atoll heat-seeking missiles. Late-model MiG-17Es had afterburning engines, but the type was transonic rather than supersonic. However, its extremely light wing-loading made it a fearsome adversary in a dogfight. Nine U.S. Navy and Marine Corps planes were lost to 17s in Vietnam, in exchange for 38 "Frescos" destroyed in the air by F-4 and F-8 pilots.

MiG-19 The 19, called "Farmer" in NATO terms, was rarely encountered over Vietnam. Like the 15 and 17, it was a single-seat fighter but its twin axial-flow turbojets propelled it to supersonic speeds. The main recognition feature is the conventionally-placed stabilator and wide vertical fin, in contrast to the T-tail configuration of the MiG-17. The 19 was a contemporary of the U.S. Air Force's F-100 Super Sabre, appearing in 1955. Its armament was usually two cannon and four missiles. Farmers downed two A-6s in 1967 but Navy Phantoms evened the score with a pair of MiG-19 kills in 1972.

MiG-21 This delta-wing single-engine single-seater has appeared in an astonishing number of variants since its debut in 1956. Almost as fast as the Phantom, it was seldom employed in the traditional dogfight. Rather, its speed and missile armament lent the "Fishbed" to hit-and-run tactics against formations of American aircraft. MiG-21s shot down four naval Phantoms and an RA-5 in Vietnam, but carrier-based F-4s and F-8s bagged 16 MiG-21s in exchange.

Champlin Fighter Museum
Falcon Field
4636 Fighter Aces Drive
Mesa, Arizona 85205

(602) 830-4540

THE CHAMPLIN FIGHTER MUSEUM

The Champlin Fighter Museum ranks as one of the world's unique historical institutions. Unlike most museums, it is privately operated, owing its origin to Douglas L. Champlin, a long-time collector of vintage aircraft. Champlin began acquiring WW II fighters in 1969 and opened his museum in Mesa, Arizona (25 miles east of Phoenix) in January 1981. With addition of original and reproduction WW I aircraft, the collection includes some 30 historic airplanes representing five nations. Most are maintained in air-worthy condition.

Designated official home of the American Fighter Aces Association in 1982, the museum hopes to add jet aircraft of Korean and Vietnam War vintage. CFM Press has begun a series of volumes which will cover the history of the men and machines which have made fighter aviation a subject of enduring fascination.

Other CFM books in print:

Big Friend, Little Friend Lt. Col. Richard E. Turner, USAF (Ret)
The Champlin Fighter Museum Coloring Book Bob Stevens, artist
America's First Eagles Lt. Lucien H. Thayer (co-published with
                                 Bender Publishing, San Jose, California)

Forthcoming titles include:

The 355th Fighter Group in WW II Bill Marshall (son of a 355th ace)
The Austro-Hungarian Aces of WW I Dr. Martin O'Connor

ABOUT THE AUTHOR

Born in Los Angeles on December 8, 1941, Randall Cunningham, Jr. grew up in Missouri. He graduated from the University of Missouri in 1964 with a bachelor's degree, taking a master's in education the following year.

A highly successful swimming coach, Cunningham produced 36 high school All-Americans in 1965-67, three of whom went on to win Olympic gold or silver medals.

"Duke" Cunningham joined the Navy in 1967 and was designated a Naval Aviator in 1968. His operational training in F-4 Phantoms began at NAS Miramar near San Diego that same year, and he joined Fighter Squadron 96 soon thereafter.

Cunningham's first combat deployment was the 1969-70 cruise of USS *America*. His second WestPac tour, the subject of this book, saw him emerge as the first American ace of the war, the first all-missile ace and the first ace mounted on the F-4.

In all, then-Lieutenant Cunningham flew 300 combat missions and was awarded the Navy Cross, two Silver Stars, 15 Air Medals and the Purple Heart. He was also decorated by the South Vietnamese government.

Subsequent assignments have included a tour as instructor at the Navy Fighter Weapons School (Top Gun), two stints with VF-154, and a post on the staff of Commander Seventh Fleet. In January 1984, this volume's publication date, Commander Cunningham became executive officer of VF-126, the Navy's west coast aggressor squadron. In all, he has flown a dozen jet fighter types and a variety of civilian aircraft. His favorite remains the Pitts S-2 aerobatic plane.

Randy Cunningham makes his home in San Diego with his wife, Nancy, and three children.

ABOUT THE AUTHOR

J eff Ethell, the son of a U.S. Air Force fighter pilot, learned to fly before he learned to drive a car. His writing career began with the National Air and Space Museum as recipient of several research grants on historic aircraft. He is a commercial pilot with multi-engine, instrument and flight instructor ratings, and has logged over 2,000 flying hours in well over 100 aircraft types. Among the military aircraft he has flown are the P-51, B-17, B-25 of WW II and current jets such as the A-4, F-4, F-15 and Harrier.

Jeff has written over 20 aviation books and hundreds of magazine articles specializing in military subjects. His previous books include *Me-163 Komet, P-38 Lightning at War, Mustang: a Documentary History, Target Berlin, F-15 Eagle, B-52 Stratofortress, The German Jets in Combat, Pilot Maker* and an extensive recounting of the Falklands War entitled *Air War South Atlantic*. The hallmark of his work is an ability to view events from the cockpits on both sides, with extensive historical documentation.

ABOUT THE COVER ILLUSTRATION

1400 HOURS , 10 MAY 1972 — After nearly five minutes of maneuvering, Randy Cunningham is beginning to roll in behind an expertly-flown MiG-17 for his third kill of the day. *Advantage Cunningham*, by Mark Waki, is a 24" x 29" limited-edition lithograph personally signed by "Duke" Cunningham and the artist. This and other prints by Mark and Matthew Waki are available from Aviation Illustrators, 353 Scott Avenue, Salt Lake City, Utah, 84115. Signed prints include U.S. Air Force ace Steve Ritchie and Medal of Honor recipient Leo Thorsness.

INDEX

Abbreviations: A/F=Airfield AFB=Air Force Base
NAS=Naval Air Station NVN=North Vietnam
PI=Philippine Islands SVN=South Vietnam